Audio Access Included

GUITAR
for Ukulele Players
by Chad Johnson

To access audio visit:
www.halleonard.com/mylibrary

Enter Code
1918-4344-4876-0059

ISBN 978-1-4803-8458-3

HAL•LEONARD®
CORPORATION
7777 W. BLUEMOUND RD. P.O. BOX 13819 MILWAUKEE, WI 53213

Visit Hal Leonard Online at
www.halleonard.com

TABLE OF CONTENTS

INTRODUCTION

Welcome to *Guitar for Ukulele Players*. Ever since the ukulele's huge comeback over the past few decades, the number of ukesters has grown to an unprecedented amount. While it used to be much more likely that a guitar player would want to add the uke to his or her stable of instruments, it's now reached a point where the opposite is not only practical—it's worthy of an instructional book! The good news for all you uke players out there is that your favorite instrument shares a great deal in common with its larger-bodied cousin. Therefore, hopefully you'll find the transition to be fun and fairly easy. That's the aim of this book!

Along the way, we'll try to highlight the similarities between the two intruments so you won't feel as though you're starting from scratch. In fact, with regards to chords and scales, you'll be able to apply and/or adapt almost all of your uke knowledge to the guitar. The main area that will demand the most effort will be on the technical side—i.e., the larger scale, the extra strings and different string tension, the adaptation of the pick (unless you use a pick on the uke), etc. But have no fear—with a healthy uke skill set under your belt, you've got a great start on the guitar. So let's stop blabbing and start strumming!

A BRIEF HISTORY LESSON

Though the ukulele was developed in Hawaii during the late 1880s as a variation of several Portuguese instruments (the machete, cavaquinho, and rajao), the guitar has a bit of a longer pedigree. Its roots can be traced back to 12th-century Europe, as it shares many traits with the lute, which describes a large family of stringed instruments from that period. The modern classical guitar (and variations thereof), which is strung with nylon ("catgut"—usually sheep intestine—back in the day) strings, began to appear most notably in Spain by the late 16th century.

By the mid-to-late 1800s, the dimensions of the Spanish classical guitar had been standardized to what we see today. About the same time, the steel-string acoustic guitar was gaining popularity, as its increased volume helped it compete with the mandolin, which had also been enjoying a popular resurgence. Not to mention, steel strings were cheaper to make, lasted longer, and stayed in tune better than catgut strings. Then, during the 1930s, the electric guitar first appeared in its infancy and the music world would never be the same. By the 1950s, the solid-body electric guitar arrived and all but took over the rock 'n' roll airwaves. However, the acoustic guitar has never been outshined and the two live peacefully, side by side, in the world of popular music to this day.

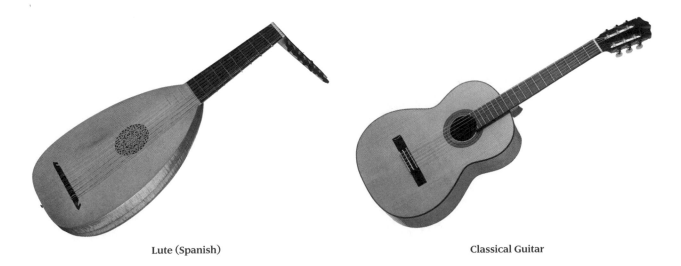

Lute (Spanish)   Classical Guitar

SAY HELLO TO THE GUITAR

You'll no doubt recognize many of these names from the ukulele, as the guitar functions and is constructed in a similar manner:

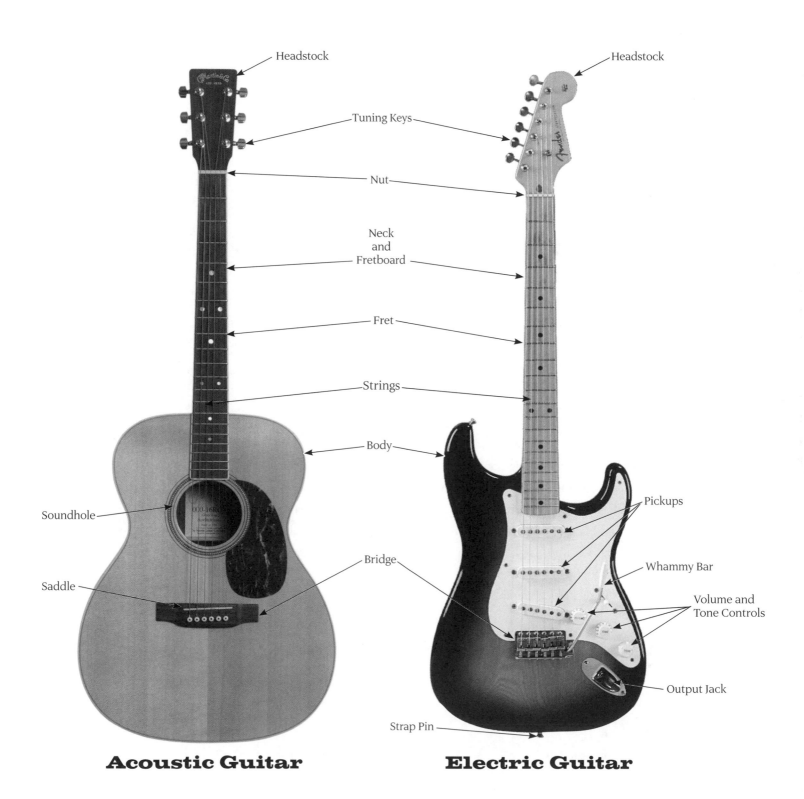

Acoustic Guitar   **Electric Guitar**

EQUIPMENT CONCERNS: CHOICES, CHOICES, CHOICES

Just as with choosing your first uke (size, acoustic vs. electric, etc.), there are some choices you'll need to make on the guitar front, too.

ACOUSTIC OR ELECTRIC?

The first choice you have to make is whether you want to play the acoustic or electric guitar. The good news is that just about everything you learn on one kind can easily be applied to the other. So, it's not a supercritical decision or anything!

Here are some factors to consider that will help you make your decision:

- **Cost:** Generally speaking, you'll spend a little more on an electric guitar setup because you'll also need an amplifier.

- **Portability:** You can't beat an acoustic guitar for campfires! Portable, battery-operated amplifiers exist too, so you can take an electric anywhere as well, but it's still not fully self-contained like the acoustic.

- **Type of Music:** If heavy metal is your thing, the acoustic is probably not the way to go. On the other hand, you don't see too many classical players wielding a Les Paul. So think about the music you'd most like to play and identify what's more common in that style.

- **Ease of Play:** An electric guitar is generally a little easier on the fingers than an acoustic guitar is, so some people choose to start on it because of that. However, if you've played uke for a while, you probably have developed some calluses already, so this may not be as much of a concern for you.

ACOUSTIC GUITARS

If you go with an acoustic guitar, the two main categories to consider are classical (nylon-string) or steel-string. Classical guitars are certainly easier on your fingers—they'll feel very similar to your uke strings—but they're not as commonly used in pop music. The typical jangly acoustic sound you hear on most songs is the steel-string acoustic guitar.

The classical guitar is a fairly standard size, but the steel-string is available in several sizes: jumbo, dreadnought, folk, etc. Each one is most commonly associated with a particular style of music, but as there are no rules in this regard, you should really try playing a variety to see which feels and sounds the best to you.

It should also be noted that nearly all of these will be available as *acoustic-electric* varieties, which means they'll have some kind of pickup or internal microphone installed. This will allow you to plug in and amplify your acoustic guitar. If you plan on jamming with a band, this might be a necessity.

Martin D-28 (dreadnought style)

Gibson J-200 (jumbo style)

ELECTRIC GUITARS

Electric guitars are the obvious choice if you really want to rock out. While electric designs get much wilder than in the acoustic varieties, sonically speaking, once again, there are two broad categories: the *Gibson style* and the *Fender style*, or the humbucker sound and the single-coil sound, respectively.

These differences relate to the type of pickups used in the guitar. Gibson is more associated with the humbucking pickup, whereas Fender is more associated with the single-coil. What's the difference? Humbucking pickups are less prone to noise interference (slight humming or buzzing), and they sound darker and a little beefier. Single-coil pickups are a little noisier and sound thinner and jangly. Both types are featured prominently in blues and rock styles. Beyond that (and there are numerous exceptions), humbuckers are often heard in hard rock, metal, and jazz styles, whereas single-coils are featured in country, funk, and surf styles.

Gibson Les Paul (with humbucking pickups)   **Fender Stratocaster (with single-coil pickups)**

AMPLIFIERS

Guitar amplifiers come in two main categories: *tube amps* and *solid state/modeling amps*. Tube amps use actual vacuum tubes in their circuitry, which means they require occasional maintenance and service (such as replacing a tube when it goes bad and/or "biasing" the amp so the tubes run at optimum current). This servicing is usually handled by a repairman. They're generally preferred by most professional players for their superior tone, but they're usually heavier and more expensive than modeling amps.

Modeling amps generally don't require servicing—though there are some "hybrid" amps that combine tubes with solid-state technology—and, as long as nothing breaks internally, they'll always sound the same. They are also more versatile, as they use digital technology to "model" the sound of classic (mostly) tube amps. It's not uncommon for one of these amps to have 10 or more models—which will alter the sound of the amp greatly—from which to choose. They also commonly have built-in effects (see Effects on page 11) which is convenient, as well. Though they are used by some professionals and/or weekend warriors on stage, they are exceptional practice amps for home because of their relatively low cost and versatility.

Fender Twin Reverb (tube amp)   **Line 6 Spider IV 75 (solid-state modeling amp)**

ACCESSORIES

There are several other goodies to go along with your guitar, as well. Some are essential, some are convenient, and some are just fun.

Cables

If you're playing electric guitar, you'll need a guitar cable. These range in length from 10 feet upwards, so make sure you get one that's long enough. If you're using an effects pedal (see next page), you'll need two: one from your guitar to the pedal, and one from the pedal to the amp.

Capos

One very common accessory in the acoustic guitar world—especially if you plan on strumming and singing songs—is a *capo*. It acts like a moveable nut, which allows you to play the same open chord shapes (which you'll be learning soon!) in various keys by clamping it down on different frets.

A spring-loaded *quick-change* style is, as you may have guessed, quicker, but the tension is not adjustable. On inexpensive models, sometimes the spring is wound a bit too tight, which means the capo will clamp the strings a little tighter than needed, pulling them sharp just a bit. A *screw-tension* type allows you to adjust the amount of tension on the clamp, which usually results in more accurate tuning. The drawback is that it can take dozens of seconds instead of just a few to change frets. If you're playing by yourself, this isn't a big deal. But when you're with a band, you'll want to watch for projectiles thrown your way if you're taking too long!

Kyser Quick-Change capo

Shubbs Original C-series capo

Picks

Picks come in all shapes, sizes, colors, and thicknesses. Most of them are held between your thumb and finger, but there are also thumb-picks, which you wear around your thumb. The bottom line is that you should just try out a bunch (they are cheap) and see which you kind like best.

Effects Pedals

These are more commonly used with electric guitar. They do things like add reverb (reverberation), delay (echo), tremolo (throbbing of volume), distortion, etc. to your signal to make it a bit more interesting and colorful. You can string together several different pedals in a row to create your own custom sound and there are a million to choose from!

| BOSS DD-3 Digital Delay pedal | Dunlop Jimi Hendrix Fuzz Face (distortion) pedal | Voodoo Lab Tremolo pedal |

TUNING THE GUITAR

The guitar has six strings. From the lowest-pitched (thickest, or 6th) string to the highest-pitched (thinnest, or 1st) string, they're tuned to the following pitches:

E – A – D – G – B – E

(Just as with the ukulele, alternate tunings for the guitar exist as well, but that's beyond the scope of this book.)

There are two main methods you can use to tune the guitar: *tuning by ear* (relative tuning) or *using an electronic tuner*.

USING AN ELECTRONIC TUNER

An electronic tuner is a device that will listen to the pitch of a guitar string and let you know whether the pitch is sharp (too high) or flat (too low). They come in several different styles, but the three main types are pedal, tabletop, and clip-on. You'll need a cable to plug into the pedal style. The tabletop style will work with a cable, but they'll often have a built-in microphone for use with acoustic guitars. The clip-on style simply clamps down on your headstock (even on an electric guitar) and senses the pitch by the vibration only.

| TC Electronic Polytune 2 pedal tuner | Korg Clip-on tuner | Korg CA-1 Chromatic tuner (tabletop style) |

Most tuners nowadays are *chromatic,* which means they'll recognize and identify any note you play. For example, if your low E string is tuned very low, down to the note D for instance, a chromatic tuner will indicate that. However, a *non-chromatic* tuner will only show the notes of the open strings (E, A, D, etc.) and won't let you know how far a string is detuned. It will only let you know that you're flat or sharp relative to each pitch. This isn't usually a problem unless you're using a capo. Since a capo changes the pitch of each string, a non-chromatic tuner won't allow you to tune the strings when a capo is on.

Using an electronic tuner is pretty straightforward. You pluck a string and the tuner will tell you whether the note needs to be raised or lowered. When the string is in tune, the tuner will usually indicate that by a change in color, two arrows pointing inward, or something similar.

Tuner reading a note as "in-tune"

TUNING BY EAR (RELATIVE TUNING)

If you don't have an electronic tuner, you can still tune the guitar by ear. This process is known as relative tuning. It's an important skill to develop even if you own and use a tuner because it helps to strengthen your ear (sense of pitch). Here's how it works:

1. Try to find a reference pitch for an E note. This could be from a piano, a pitch pipe, a song that you know is in the key of E, etc. Match the pitch of your low E string to that. If you can't find a reference pitch, just tune the low E string until it seems close to you.

2. Fret the 6th string at fret 5. This will produce the note A. Tune the 5th string until it matches this pitch.

3. Fret the 5th string at fret 5. This will produce the note D. Tune the 4th string until it matches this pitch.

4. Fret the 4th string at fret 5. This will produce the note G. Tune the 3rd string until it matches this pitch.

5. Heads up! Fret the 3rd string at *fret 4.* This will produce the note B. Tune the 2nd string until it matches this pitch.

6. Fret the 2nd string at fret 5. This will produce the note E. Tune the 1st string until it matches this pitch.

When matching the pitches of two strings, allow both notes to ring together. You'll hear a series of warbles (called beats) when the strings are out of tune. The closer to "in tune" the strings get, the slower the beats will become. Once the beats stop, the strings are in tune.

TUNING TIP!

When matching the pitch of another string, it's best to tune up to it rather than down. In other words, if you pluck the open string and find that it's sharp (i.e., higher in pitch than the fretted note), first bring the pitch down to where it's slightly flat and then tune it back up to pitch. It's also helpful to stretch the strings a bit before tuning. Place your thumb and fingers along one string and pinch your fingers toward your palm to stretch them. Both of these tips will help your strings stay in tune better.

 For your convenience, there are tuning notes provided with the accompanying audio. If you don't have a tuner or a pitch reference available, you can use it to get tuned up!

DON'T MISS!

The first four strings on the guitar (strings 4 thru 1) are tuned the same way as your uke; they're just a 4th interval lower in pitch. If you place a capo on fret 5 of the guitar, the pitches from string 4 to string 1 will be the same as your uke: G–C–E–A. The only difference is that the G wouldn't be up an octave as it is in reentrant tuning on the uke. This is great news as you'll see when it comes time to learn chords!

HOLDING, PICKING, AND FRETTING THE GUITAR

OK, you're in tune and ready to rock! So how do you play this thing? It's time to take a look at guitar technique.

TO STAND OR TO SIT?

Most people practice sitting down, but many perform standing up. If you think you'll ever play on stage (or anywhere) standing, you should definitely get used to the way it feels before stepping out in front of the audience. If you've never had that experience, it can be quite unsettling! For this reason, I'd recommend getting comfortable playing in both positions.

Sitting

One common sitting position involves resting the guitar on your right leg (for a right-handed player) with your knees bent at close to a 90-degree angle. This usually requires a chair or stool that's slightly lower than normal seating height (unless you're fairly tall). You want to avoid having to hunch over the guitar.

Alternatively, you can rest the guitar on the left leg and use a footstool to increase the angle of the neck a bit. This is the preferred position for classical players, but it's used by many others as well. It puts the neck in a very comfortable playing position.

Standing

While many uke players simply cradle the uke with their forearm while standing, this is not recommended with a guitar. Therefore, you'll need to use a guitar strap when you stand. Almost all electric guitars have strap pins for this purpose; many acoustic guitars do too. If your guitar doesn't have them, you can get them installed cheaply. (See the picture for proper placement of the strap.)

Though the rockers like to wear the guitar around their kneecaps, this does not make for a comfortable position! Besides the fact that it forces you to overarch your wrist, which could lead to injury, you'll be forced to hunch forward more to see the fretboard. Ideally, the guitar should hang at relatively the same position as when you're seated. If you feel compelled to loosen the strap for the sake of the show, feel free, but be warned! The guitar will feel very different, so be sure to practice that way before hitting the stage!

THE PICK HAND

Although most uke players strum and pluck with bare fingers, it's most common to use a plectrum (flatpick or pick) with the guitar. (Many guitarists do use their bare fingers as well, so don't think of this as a steadfast rule.) To hold the pick, place it between your thumb and index finger so that it rests against the first joint of the index finger. It should be held firmly enough that it doesn't slip out of your grip but not so tight that it feels rigid.

A *thumb-pick* is shaped with a loop that fastens around your thumb. These are common among some country players (Chet Atkins used a thumb-pick), but they can be used in all styles if desired. They allow you to achieve a pick sound with your thumb while using your fingers in conjunction on the higher strings for more intricate, fingerstyle picking. You can also use them as a flatpick, which means they're quite versatile. They will feel a bit different than a standard flatpick, though, so it may take a bit of getting used to.

Strumming

Strumming with a pick shouldn't feel too awkward, as the motion is basically the same as used when playing the uke; the motion mostly comes from the wrist. It's usually best to slightly angle the pick so that the front edge (edge closest to the guitar neck) makes contact with the string first, as this will allow it to glide through the strings easier. One minor difference is that, while the uke is often strummed near the neck/body joint, the guitar is normally strummed a bit farther toward the bridge. On an acoustic, this normally means roughly over the center of the soundhole. However, feel free to adjust this as you see fit. The closer you move toward the bridge, the brighter the sound becomes.

Picking

When playing single notes with a pick, try to minimize your hand motion so your hand doesn't lift up from the guitar. It's a combination of wrist movement and a little bit of forearm movement. As with strumming the uke, both downstrokes and upstrokes are used. To get a feel for this, try slowly alternating between a downward pick and upward pick on the open low E string. Remember: think economy of motion. After picking the string with a downstroke, the pick should remain close to the string, ready to pick upwards if need be.

NOTATION AND TAB PRIMER

You may have learned to read music on the uke, but if not, no sweat. We'll run through the basics here for you and then you should be able to pick it up as we move through the book.

THE STAFF

Guitar music is written on a staff. It uses a treble clef, which assigns certain notes to the lines and spaces of the staff. The notes on the five lines, from low to high, are E–G–B–D–F. You can think: **E**very **G**ood **B**oy **D**oes **F**ine. The four spaces are even easier. From low to high, they are F–A–C–E, or "FACE." Notice that, when you progress up through the lines and spaces, you move straight through the alphabet. The musical alphabet only uses the letters A–G; after that, it starts over.

The Staff

When notes need to go higher or lower than the staff, we add temporary ledger lines.

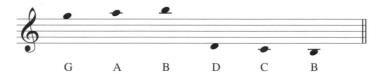

RHYTHMS

Music is divided into *measures* (or bars) to make it easier to read. A *time signature* tells us how many beats are in each measure (top number) and what type of note will be counted as a beat (bottom number).

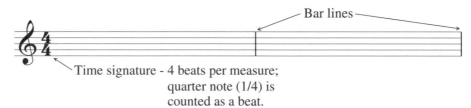

Music is written on the staff with various noteheads and stems to indicate the rhythm.

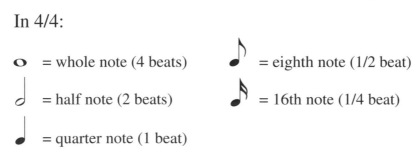

When no note is to be played, rests are used to indicate silence.

In 4/4:

➖ = whole rest (4 beats)   𐄇 = eighth rest (1/2 beat)

➖ = half rest (2 beats)   𐄇 = 16th rest (1/4 beat)

𝄽 = quarter rest (1 beat)

When several eighth or 16th notes appear in a row, they're *beamed* together.

SHORTCUTS AND OTHER SYMBOLS

A *key signature* is a collection of sharps or flats at the beginning of a piece that lets the performer know that every time a certain note arises, it's to be played as a sharp or flat note. In the old days, this saved the copyist from having to rewrite the same accidentals (sharps or flats) over and over again. This also identifies the key of a piece of music. Just as there are 12 different keys on a piano keyboard within one octave (or from one C to the next, for example), there are 12 different key signatures.

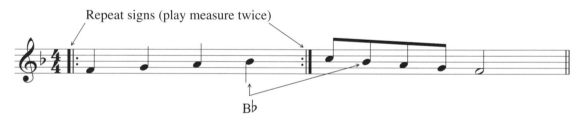

Repeat signs tell you to repeat the enclosed material before continuing.

Bracketed endings tell you to repeat a piece of music but use one ending the first time and a second ending the second time. In the example below, you would play measures 1 thru 4 and then repeat from the beginning. The second time through, you'd skip measure 4 and go straight to measure 5, continuing on from there.

TABLATURE (TAB)

You may or may not have come across tab in your uke studies. *Tablature* (or *tab* for short) is another way of notating music for fretted instruments. In tab, the six lines represent the six strings of the guitar; the lowest line corresponds to the 6th string (thickest) of the guitar, and the highest line the 1st string (thinnest). A number on a line tells you which fret to play on what string. A "o" indicates an open (unfretted) string.

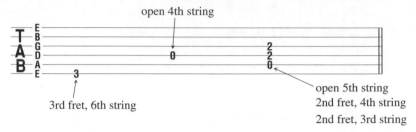

open 4th string

3rd fret, 6th string

open 5th string
2nd fret, 4th string
2nd fret, 3rd string

In this book, as is often the case with guitar music, tab is used in conjunction with standard notation. This is ideal because, whereas the standard notation supplies the rhythms that are missing in the tab, the tab will show exactly where to play a certain note on the neck (many times, the same note can be played at several different places on a guitar neck).

CHORD GRIDS

The chords in this book are also written as *chord grids*. In case you didn't come across these handy little guys in your time with the uke, here's how you read them:

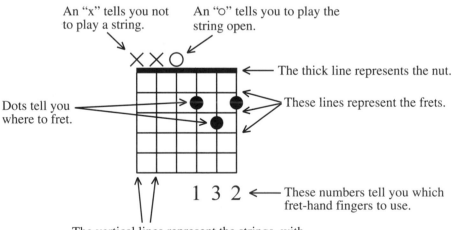

An "x" tells you not to play a string.

An "o" tells you to play the string open.

The thick line represents the nut.

These lines represent the frets.

Dots tell you where to fret.

These numbers tell you which fret-hand fingers to use.

The vertical lines represent the strings, with string 6 (thickest) on the left and string 1 (thinnest) on the right.

CHAPTER 1: E MINOR AND A MINOR CHORDS

One of the best benefits of playing both the uke and the guitar is that the chords you learned on uke won't be in vain. Just about every chord shape you learned on uke will be applicable on the first four strings of the guitar. However, because the guitar is tuned lower than the uke, they'll sound at a different pitch, but at least your fingers will be somewhat acclimated to the shapes.

E MINOR (Em)

Let's look at your first guitar chord: Em. This one requires only two fingers, so it's a good one to start with. Place your second finger on string 5, fret 2 and your third finger on string 4, fret 2. Strum through all six strings.

Em

2 3

Check out the first four strings. Recognize that shape? That's right! This chord corresponds to the Am shape on the uke:

Am

Let's hear the Em chord in action. Strum the chord gracefully and deliberately with a smooth downstroke (toward the floor). Try to milk all the sadness from it that you can!

E MINOR HEARTBREAK

Now let's incorporate a little more strumming. You'll use downstrokes (⊓) primarily, but for the eighth notes, you'll use a downstroke followed immediately by an upstroke (V). Aim to make the pick glide smoothly through the strings.

TURNING UP THE HEAT

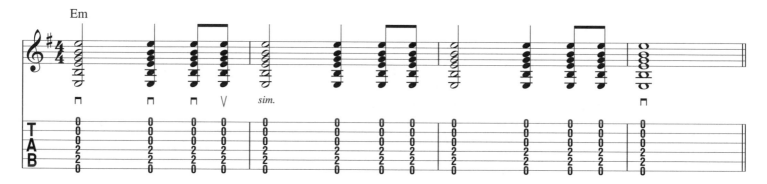

Now let's add another chord to your arsenal.

A MINOR (Am)

Our second chord, Am, requires three fingers. Place your second finger on string 4, fret 2, your third finger on string 3, fret 2, and your first finger on string 2, fret 1. Strum the first five strings.

You should recognize this shape as Dm on the uke:

Remember to use an upstroke for the last eighth note in each measure!

JUST A MINOR THING

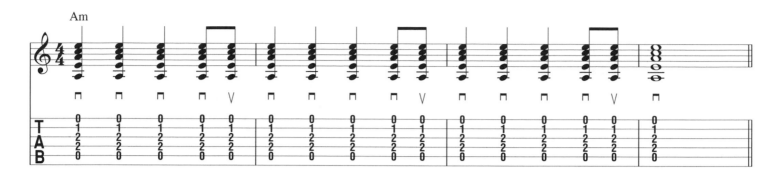

And now let's try moving between these two chords. Notice that your second and third fingers are orientated the same way in both chords. You should use this to your advantage when changing between the two. Try to move those two fingers as one unit.

BACK AND FORTH

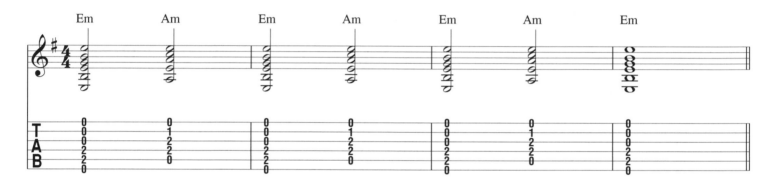

CHAPTER 2: G MAJOR AND C MAJOR CHORDS

OK, let's balance things out a bit now by learning some major chords.

G MAJOR (G)

There are actually several different ways to play an open G chord, and they're all quite common. What is used really depends on the individual. So we're going to look at each one, then you can decide which feels best to you. For each option, you'll be strumming through all six strings.

Option 1

This is fairly easy on the fret hand. Place your second finger on fret 3, string 6, your first finger on fret 2, string 5, and your third finger on fret 3, string 1. Strum through all six strings.

If you look at the first four strings of this shape, you should recognize it as the C major chord shape on the uke:

Option 2

This is the same exact G chord as option 1, but we're using different fingers. Place your third finger on fret 3, string 6, your second finger on fret 2, string 5, and your fourth finger on fret 3, string 1. This is a bit more of a stretch, and you'll certainly feel the larger scale of the guitar (as compared to the uke) with this one. However, the benefit of this fingering is that it enables you to decorate the chord by adding various notes with your first finger, and it's also very handy for switching between G and C (as you'll soon see).

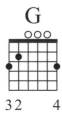

Option 3

This version actually uses a different note than the other chord, but it's still a G major chord. The fingering here is pretty easy. Place your second finger on fret 3, string 6, your first finger on fret 2, string 5, your third finger on fret 3, string 2, and your fourth finger on fret 3, string 1.

C MAJOR (C)

Now let's take a look at the C chord. This one is a bit of a stretch too compared to the uke's cramped quarters. Place your third finger on fret 3, string 5, your second finger on fret 2, string 4, and your first finger on fret 1, string 2. You'll only strum strings 5 thru 1 for this chord.

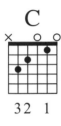

Looking at the first four strings of this shape, you should recognize it as an F major chord shape on the uke:

DON'T MISS!

Have you noticed a pattern between the guitar and uke chord shapes? Each uke chord is four letters higher than its corresponding guitar shape. In other words, C on the guitar looks like F on the uke: **C (1)** D (2) E (3) **F (4)**. Remember how we said earlier that the guitar is tuned a 4th interval lower than the uke? A 4th is a musical interval that corresponds to four note names.

FINGERING TIP!

It's pretty difficult to always avoid the sixth string when strumming, especially when you're strumming eighth notes or some other busy rhythm. Therefore, you can employ finger muting to help keep that string quiet. On a C chord, this can be accomplished in one of two ways:

Option A

Allow the tip of your third finger to touch the sixth string while fretting the fifth string.

Option B

Use your thumb to lightly touch the sixth string.

Both of these methods will effectively "deaden" the sixth string, which will allow you to strum without having to worry about nicking the low E string.

Let's put these two new chords to work. In this next example, we'll be incorporating *rests*, or silence. Since these chords have open strings in them, this means we'll have to do something to stop them from ringing out. This is accomplished with *muting technique*. Again, there are two different ways to do this:

Option A

After playing the chord, lay the fingers of your fret hand lightly across all the strings.

Option B

After strumming the chord, lightly lay your picking-hand palm on the strings to deaden them.

To really be sure nothing rings out, it's not a bad idea to get in the habit of using both methods at the same time.

 ## STOP AND GO

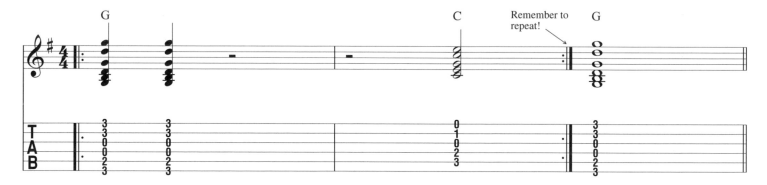

In examples like the one above, you have a lot of time between chord changes, so fingering isn't a big concern. But with less time to change chords, it becomes a bigger issue. In this next example, we're moving between G and C again, but we have less time to make the change. Therefore, we're employing Option 2 of the G chord because of its close resemblance to the C chord fingering. Notice that your third and second fingers only need to shift over one string; their relative placement within each chord is the same. Watch out for the eighth notes in the strumming pattern; you'll use a downstroke/upstroke combination for those!

"GEE," I CAN "SEE" IT NOW

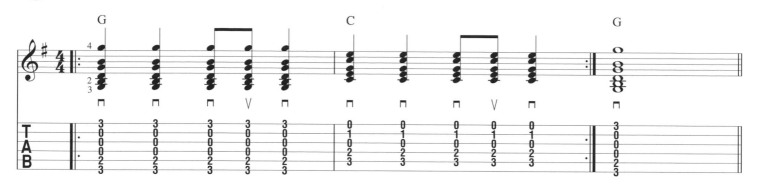

Now let's take another look at this common fingering approach. In this example, we're going to mix a major chord with a minor chord: G and Em. If you use the Option 2 fingering for G and compare it to Em, do you notice anything? (Hint: Look closely at your second finger!) Yes! Your second finger is in the same exact spot for both chords. This is called a *common tone*, and it can really help to make the chord change much smoother. When changing from G to Em, there's no reason to lift all of your fingers off of the neck. Keep that second finger in place and use it as a guide.

SMOOTH TWO-CHORD CHANGE

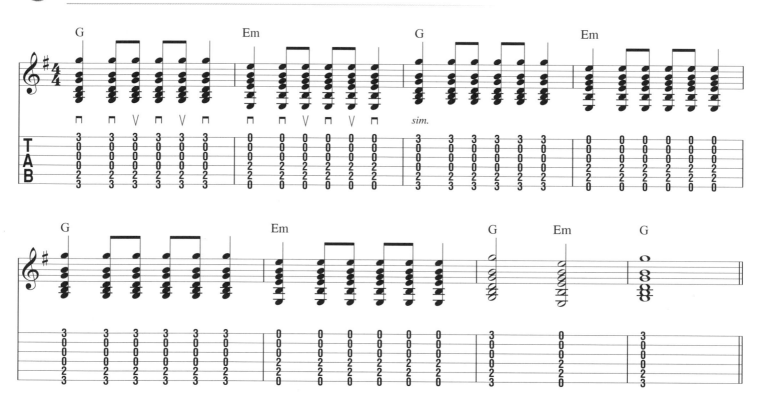

Alright! Now you know enough chords to play one of the Beatles' greatest hits, "Eleanor Rigby." There's not a lot of fancy stuff going on here, but the tempo is a little on the quick side, so that will keep you on your toes! The curved line with a dot beneath it, sitting over the final measure, is called a *fermata*. It tells you to sustain the chord (or note) indefinitely (until it fades out or until someone cues you to continue on).

ELEANOR RIGBY

Words and Music by John Lennon and Paul McCartney

Intro

Ah, _____ look at all ____ the lone - ly peo - ple.

Verse

El - ea - nor Rig - by picks up the rice ___ in a church ___ where a wed - ding has been, ___

_____ lives in a dream. ___ Waits at the win - dow, wear - ing the face ___ that she keeps ___

Now let's take a look at another song that mixes major and minor chords. This time we'll be strumming to the soulful sounds of Etta James's classic "I'd Rather Go Blind." This song is in a time signature of *12/8*. This means that there are 12 beats in a measure and the eighth note is counted as one beat.

When playing in 12/8, the eighth notes are grouped in four sets of three. So it's counted as **1** 2 3, **4** 5 6, **7** 8 9, **10** 11 12, with the first, fourth, seventh, and tenth beats receiving more stress than the others. Alternately, some people choose to count this meter as having four beats, each of which are subdivided into three. So you may hear "**one** and uh, **two** and uh, **three** and uh, **four** and uh" or "**1** 2 3, **2** 2 3, **3** 2 3, **4** 2 3."

There are two different strum patterns in this song and you have a choice in which direction you strum. Since the tempo is so slow, you can use all downstrokes without much of a problem. But you can incorporate upstrokes as well, if that feels better. Try out both of the suggestions to see which option feels better to you.

I'D RATHER GO BLIND

Words and Music by Ellington Jordan and Billy Foster

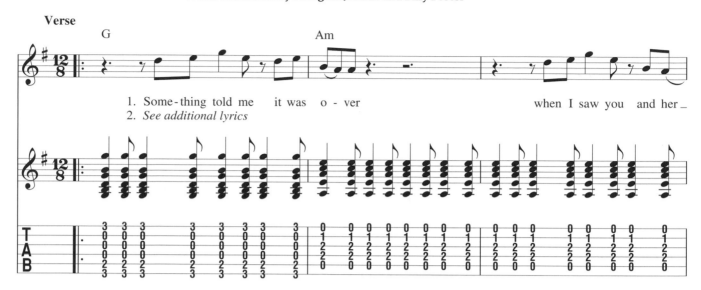

1. Some-thing told me it was o - ver when I saw you and her
2. *See additional lyrics*

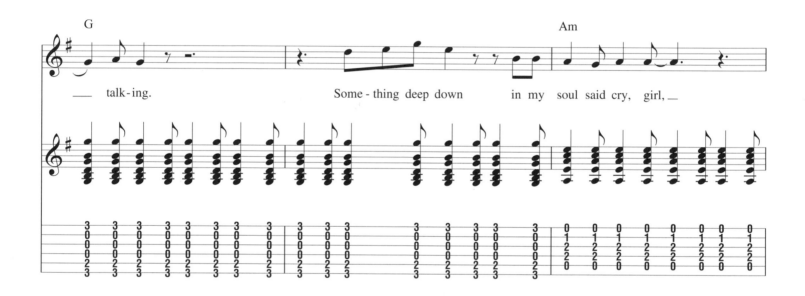

____ talk - ing. Some-thing deep down in my soul said cry, girl, ____

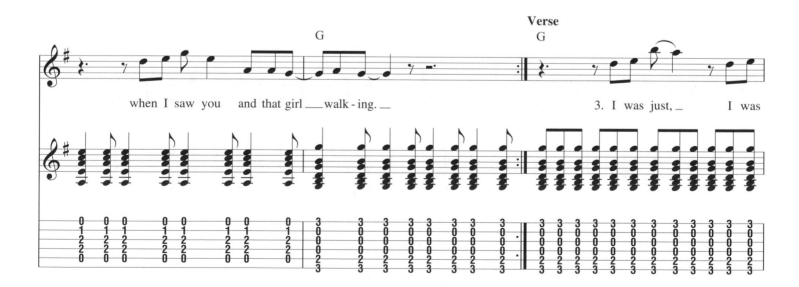

when I saw you and that girl ____ walk - ing. ____ 3. I was just, ____ I was

just, __ I was just __ sit-tin' here think-in' of your kiss and your warm __ em-brace

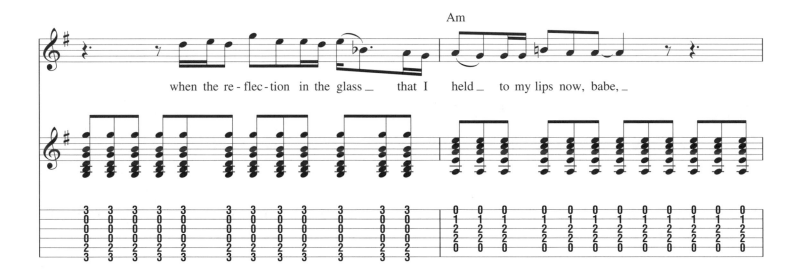

when the re - flec-tion in the glass __ that I held __ to my lips now, babe, __

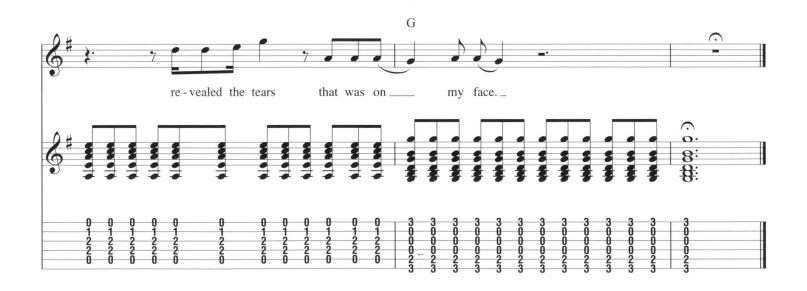

re - vealed the tears that was on _____ my face. __

Additional Lyrics

2. I would rather, I would rather go blind, boy,
Than to see you walk away from me, child.
So youn see, I love you so much that I don't wanna watch you leave me, baby.
Most of all, I just don't wanna be free.

Chapter 3: D Major, D7, A Major, and A7 Chords

Let's add a few more essential major chords to our library.

D MAJOR (D)

Place your first finger on fret 2, string 3, your third finger on fret 3, string 2, and your second finger on fret 2, string 1. Strum the first four strings.

You'll no doubt recognize this as the G major chord shape on the uke:

CHORD TIP!

On this chord, it's not fatal if you strum the fifth string by mistake because that note (A) is a strong tone of the D chord. But you really don't want to nick the low E string because it won't sound very good. (Try strumming all six strings to see what I mean.) So it's best to mute it. The easiest way to do this is with the thumb. Just bring it over the top of the neck and have it make light contact with the low E string.

Now you can strum away without worrying about hitting that string!

D7

Our D7 chord, which is a *dominant* chord, differs from D major by only one note. Place your second finger on fret 2, string 3, your first finger on fret 1, string 2, and your third finger on fret 2, string 1. Strum the first four strings.

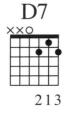

You'll recognize this as the G7 chord shape on the uke:

G7

Let's put our new D chords to work. This next example illustrates how dominant chords can add extra tension, as well as provide a strong sense of resolution, compared to major chords alone. The D chord in measure 2 wants to resolve to a G chord. However, notice that tendency increases even more when the D becomes D7 in measure 4. In this example, it's best to use your pick hand palm to mute the strings during the rests to allow your fretting hand time to grab the next chord.

THE POWER OF THE DOMINANT

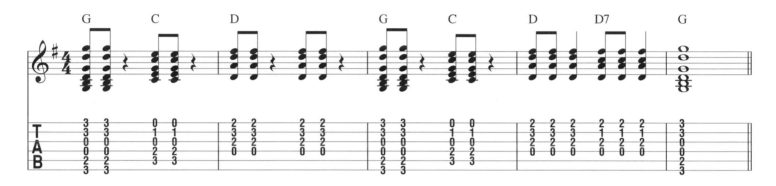

In this example, we're focusing on changing chords quickly. For each one, you'll have only an eighth note to make the switch. Depending on the tempo, this can be very quick. You'll really need to have those chord shapes down in order to make this happen!

CHUGGIN' AWAY IN E MINOR

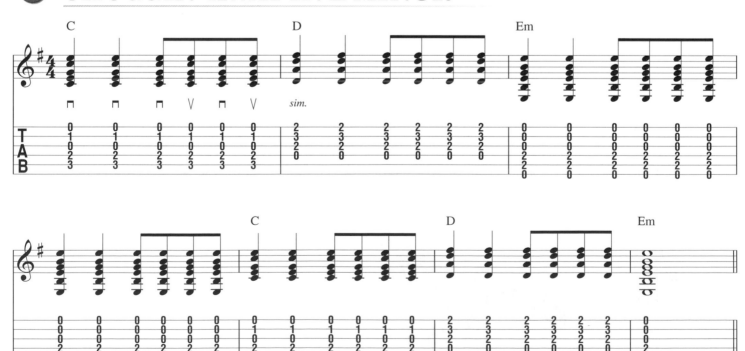

A Cheat That Won't Get You in Trouble!

At faster tempos, sometimes changing chords quickly is very difficult. In those instances, you can actually cheat a bit with an old trick that's used by all the pros at one time or another. You've probably used the same idea in your uke playing from time to time—even if you weren't aware of it! You can actually lift your fretting hand off the chord on the last eighth note to help reach the new chord in time. For that one eighth note, you'll either hear a few open strings being strummed (most likely the first few since you'll be picking with an upstroke), a few strings being muted, or a combination of the two. At moderate to faster tempos, the effect is negligible.

Check it out here as we alternate between Em and D chords.

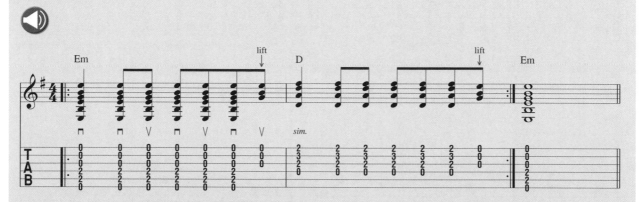

It's hard to even tell on the Em chord because it has three open strings on top anyway. If you listen closely, you can hear it on the D chord. But when you're not listening for it—or especially if there's a melody playing over the chord—it just passes right by.

Now it's time for another tune. Jimi Hendrix had a huge hit with his cover of Bob Dylan's "All Along the Watchtower." His version actually became more popular than the original! We've transposed it to the key of E minor here. You'll be changing chords within the space of an eighth note again. However, watch out for the intro. There, you'll be changing chords on the *upbeats*, which is something we haven't done yet. Once the verse starts, you'll settle into more of a normal strumming pattern.

ALL ALONG THE WATCHTOWER

Words and Music by Bob Dylan

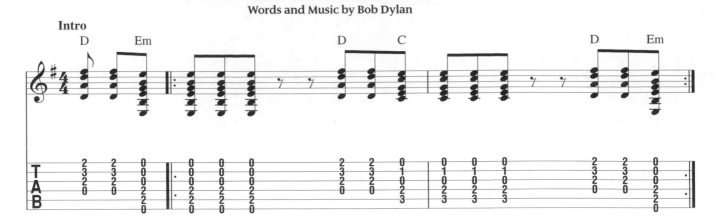

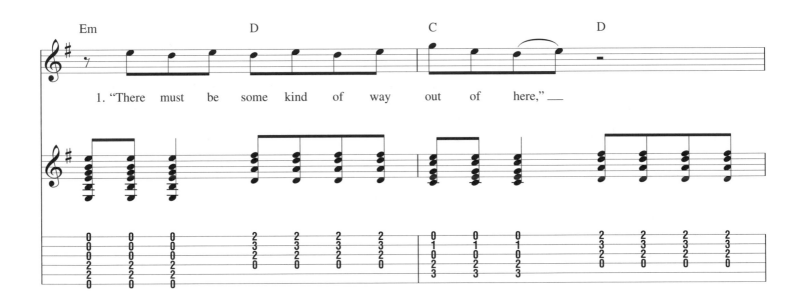

1. "There must be some kind of way out of here," ___

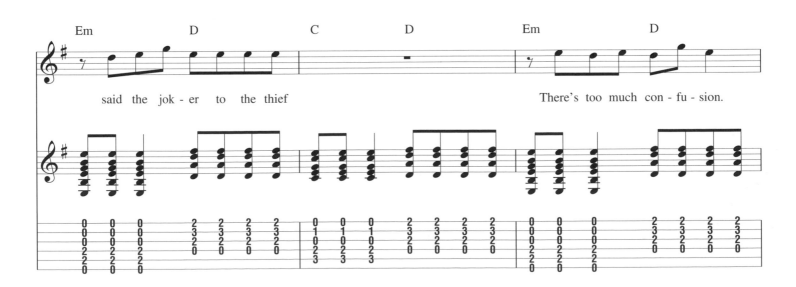

said the jok - er to the thief   There's too much con - fu - sion.

A MAJOR (A)

It's time for a new chord: A major. There are a few different fingering variations for this one, as well, so we'll look at them all.

Option 1

For the first version, place your first finger on fret 2, string 4, your second finger on fret 2, string 3, and your third finger on fret 2, string 2. Strum strings 5 thru 1.

You should recognize this shape as the D major chord on the uke:

Option 2

For the second version, place your second finger on string 4, your third finger on string 3, and your fourth finger on string 2. Some people find this fingering a bit easier than the first because it's a tight squeeze to get all three fingers in the same fret, and the pinky is usually smaller than the index finger. (Although, this is nothing compared to squeezing all those fingers together for a D chord on the uke!)

Option 3

For the final version, place your second finger on string 4, your first finger on string 3, and your third finger on string 2. Some people prefer this fingering because it keeps the first finger on string 3 when moving from A to D or from A to E (which we'll learn in Chapter 6). Both are really common chord moves.

With all of these fingerings, it's also common to mute the sixth string with the thumb. However, since the E is a strong note within an A major chord, it won't sound out of place if you occasionally nick the low E when strumming.

A7

To play A7, we only need to change one note in our A chord: we just leave string 3 open instead of playing it at fret 2. The most common fingering for A7 uses your second finger on string 4 and your third finger on string 2. However, this may change depending on the situation. For example, if you're moving from A to A7, you should simply lift your finger from string 3, regardless of the fingering you choose for A. Strum strings 5 thru 1, using your thumb to mute the low E string if necessary.

In this next example, we're making use of a tie in the second measure. These curved lines "tie" together the rhythmic values of the joined notes. This means you sustain that last D chord strum through the end of the measure. Remember: whichever fingering you use for the A chord, you can access A7 by simply lifting your finger from string 3.

TYING IT ALL TOGETHER

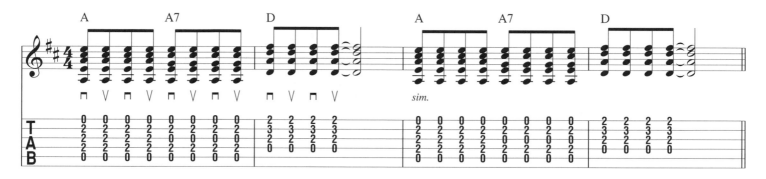

In order to help bring your strum patterns to life, it's helpful to incorporate accents. This simply means strumming some beats louder than others. You've no doubt incorporated this technique in your uke playing—consciously or not—and it's equally effective on guitar. When you see the ">" symbol below, strum a bit harder than normal. Accenting beats 2 and 4 like this is common on guitar.

NICE ACCENT!

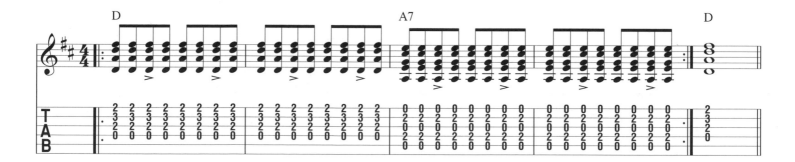

OK, let's close out this chapter with another tune. For "All Apologies," try applying a subtle accent on beats 2 and 4 as in the previous example to help move this song along. It won't hit you over the head, but you'll miss it when it's gone.

Notice that we chose to use Option 3 for the G chord. This is because it makes for an easy change when moving from D. There's a common tone on fret 3, string 2, and your third finger can remain there for both chords.

ALL APOLOGIES

Words and Music by Kurt Cobain

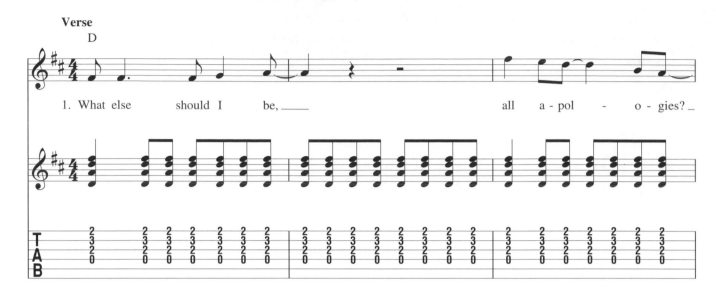

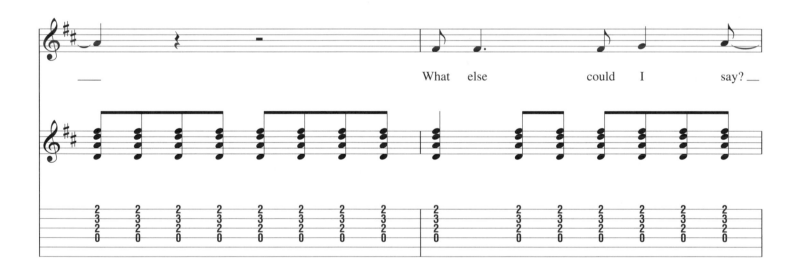

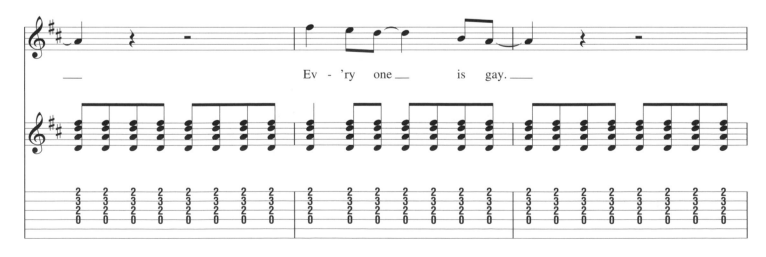

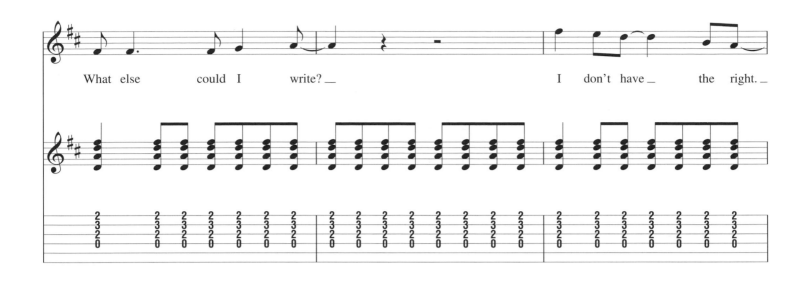

What else could I write? ___ I don't have ___ the right. ___

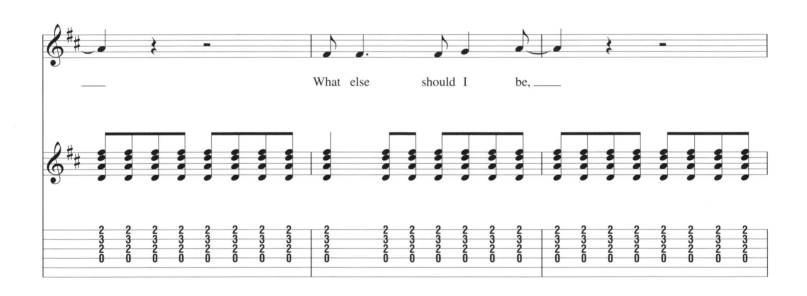

___ What else should I be, ___

Chorus
G

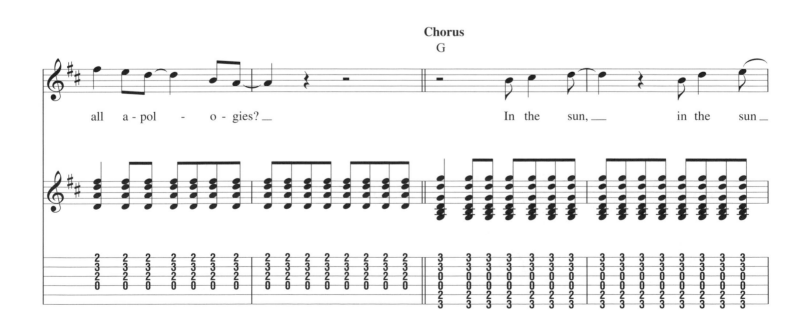

all a-pol - o - gies? ___ In the sun, ___ in the sun ___

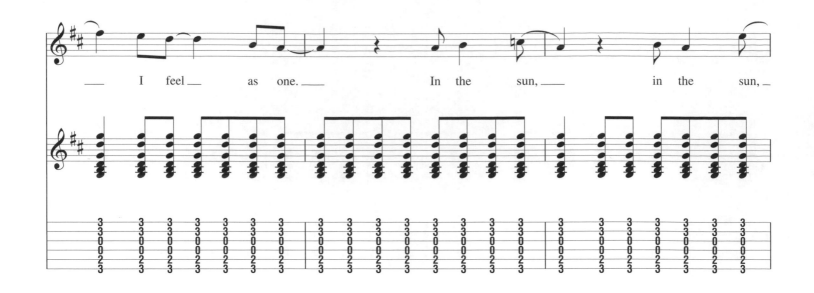

I feel ___ as one. ___ In the sun, ___ in the sun, ___

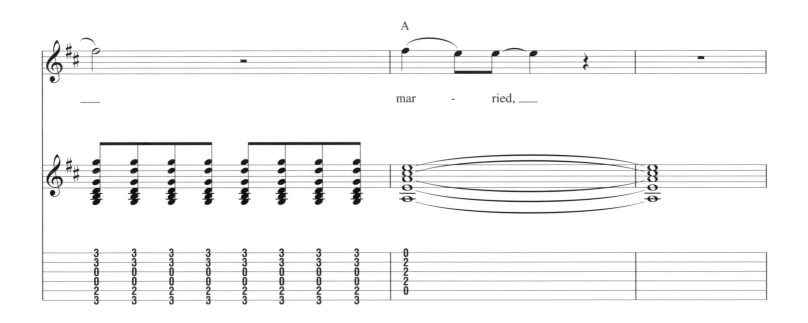

mar - ried, ___

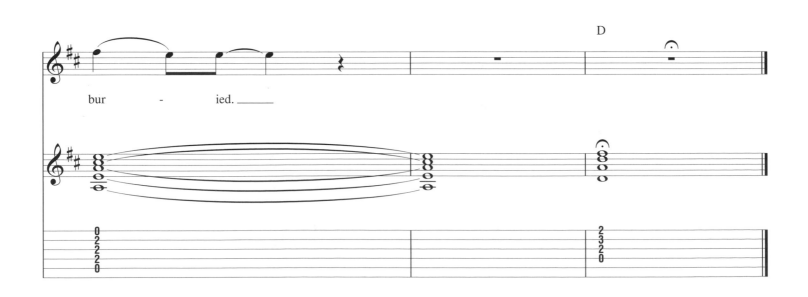

bur - ied. ___

CHAPTER 4: E MINOR PENTATONIC AND C MAJOR SCALES

Let's take a break from strumming for a bit and start playing some single notes. Remember to keep economy of motion in mind here, as well. Your pick shouldn't come very far from the string after you pluck it (unless you're trying to be really flashy or something!).

E MINOR PENTATONIC SCALE

This is one of the first things many guitar players learn to play and it's a great way to start learning some melodies. In the grid diagram below, the open circles represent the "root" of the scale. This is the note that gives the scale its name and the one that sounds resolved, or "like home." Regarding your fret hand, you should use either your first (fret 2) and second (fret 3) or your second (fret 2) and third (fret 3) fingers throughout. You don't want to be fretting every note with your index finger because that will become extremely limiting in a hurry.

You'll recognize the top part of this shape as the A minor pentatonic (or C major pentatonic) scale shape on the uke:

Am Pentatonic

PICKING TIP!

When playing single notes, unintentional noises can pop out if you're not careful. With only one finger on the fretboard, there are a lot of other strings that, if left to their own devices, can rattle and make noise. Therefore, it's a good idea to employ some muting with your pick hand to help keep this to a minimum.

When you're picking the low E string, there's nothing you can do about it. But once you move through the other strings, you can rest your palm on any lower-pitched strings that you're not picking. For example, when you're picking the D (fourth) string, your palm should be resting on strings 6 and 5 to keep them quiet.

With practice, this will become instinctual, and your palm will simply follow your pick (always one string behind it) to wherever it travels.

The E minor pentatonic scale is great for blues riffs like this one.

 ## BLUES RIFF

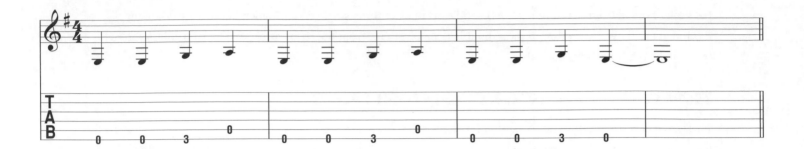

The Other Side of the Muting Coin

You may have noticed a bit of muddiness or extraneous string noise when playing the previous example. That's because your pick hand can only do so much when it comes to muting. The rest of the muting job needs to be handled by your fret hand.

When you fret the G note on fret 3, string 6, for example, you should also lightly lay your first finger across the strings behind the fretting finger. This will keep them quiet, even if they happen to be brushed with the pick or pick-hand palm. When fretting with the first finger, simply flatten it out a bit so that the underside lightly rests on the thinner strings.

You can rock out with this scale, too. Here's a cool lick that works its way through all of the strings.

 ## ROCK LICK

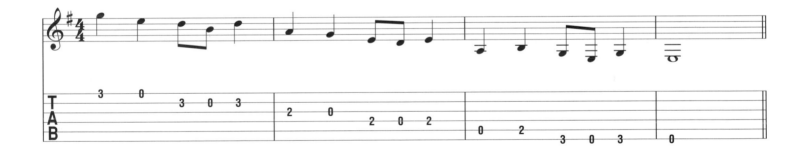

In this example, we're getting a little trickier, rhythmically. We're employing a bit of syncopation, which means we're accenting a weak beat (upbeat). Count along until you can feel it, if you need to. We're also introducing a *dotted note*. A dot increases the rhythmic value of a note by one half. In this case, a dotted quarter note is like a quarter note tied to an eighth note.

🔊 SPY ROCK

Let's put our new scale to work in a song. We've transposed Tracy Chapman's "Give Me One Reason" to the key of E and simplified the melody just a bit so you can play it with the E minor pentatonic scale. If you have trouble reading any of the rhythms, count along and/or listen to the audio until you get the feel for it.

There's a guitar solo in the middle too, so you get a chance to rock out a bit! "D.C. al Fine" stands for *Da Capo al Fine*—Italian for "start from the top and play until you see 'Fine.'"

GIVE ME ONE REASON

Words and Music by Tracy Chapman

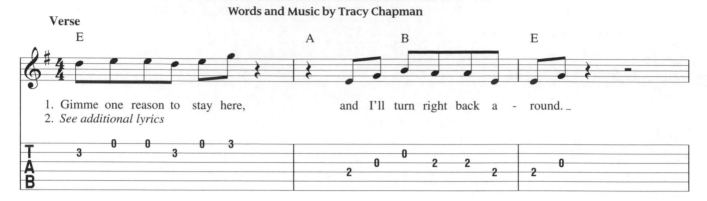

1. Gimme one reason to stay here, and I'll turn right back a - round.
2. *See additional lyrics*

Gimme one reason to stay here, and I'll turn right back a - round.

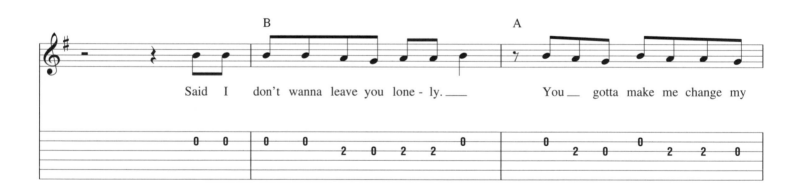

Said I don't wanna leave you lone - ly. You gotta make me change my

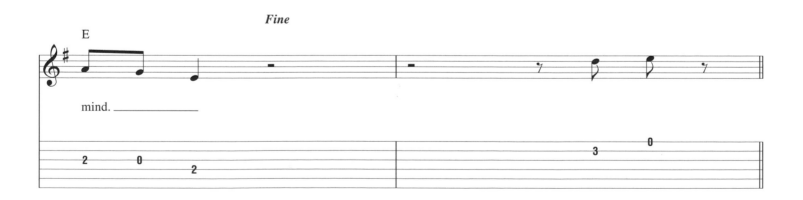

mind.

Guitar Solo

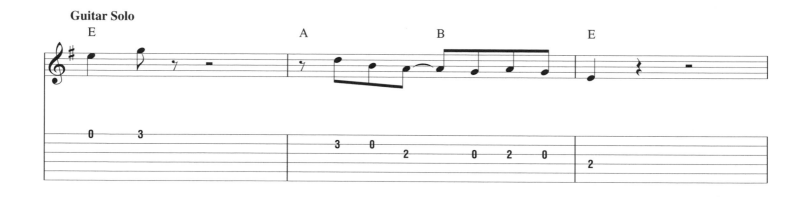

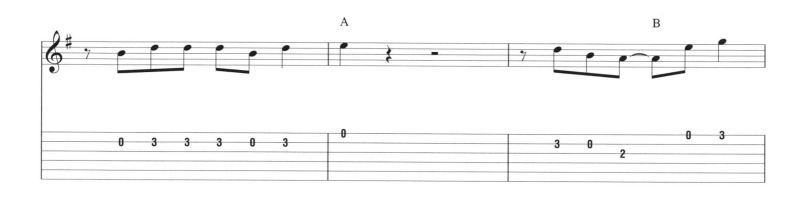

D.C. al Fine

Additional Lyrics

2. Baby, just give me one reason, give me just one reason why.
   Baby, just give me one reason, give me just one reason why I should stay.
   Because I told you that I loved you, and there ain't no more to say.

C MAJOR SCALE

Now let's look at another scale: C major. Whereas the pentatonic scale had five different notes in each octave (hence the name "penta"), the major scale has seven different notes. The C major scale contains no accidentals (sharps or flats).

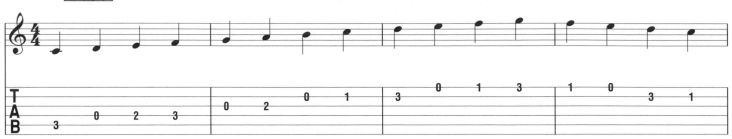

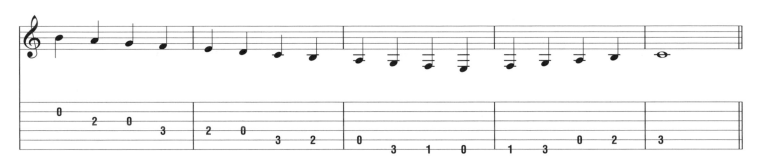

You should recognize this pattern as the F major scale on the uke:

Major Scale

Here's a cool low-register riff we can play with this scale. Remember to rest your palm on the strings and/or lift your fret-hand fingers up for the rests.

BASS RIFF

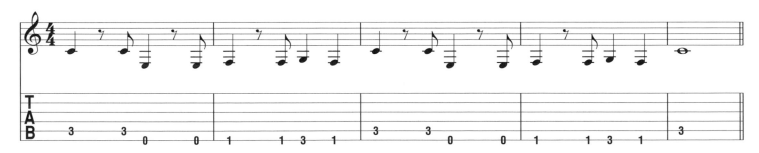

And now let's work with the higher strings of the scale. Take it slowly at first before playing along with the audio.

TREBLE RIFF

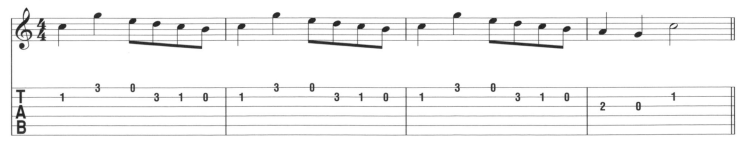

This next example is a scale sequence using the C major scale. A *sequence* is a pattern of notes that's applied throughout the scale. Sequences like this one are a great way to familiarize yourself with any scale you learn.

 ## C MAJOR SCALE SEQUENCE

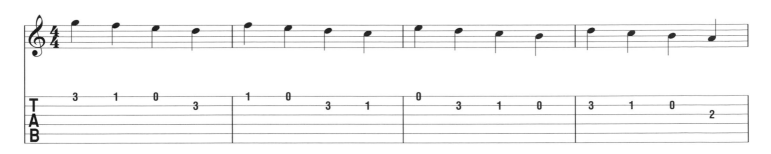

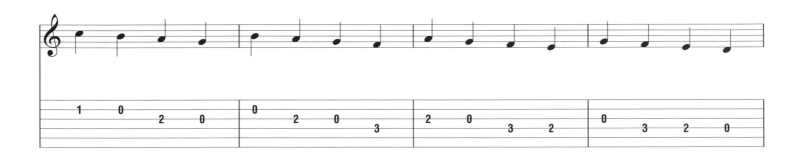

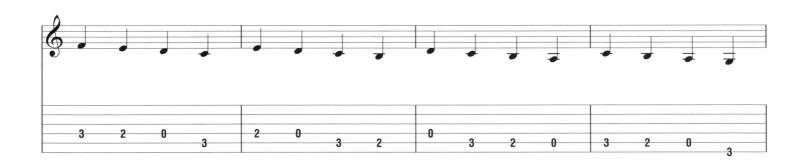

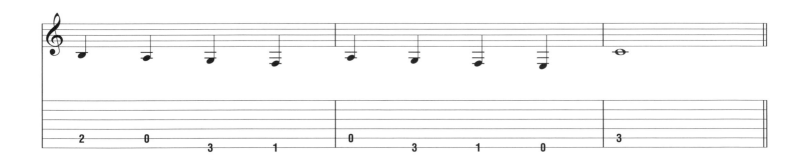

MUTING TIP!

Examples like the one above will really help you with your muting techniques because chances are you'll hear a few extraneous notes ring out. If you do, try to isolate what's happening and apply the proper muting technique (pick hand or fret hand) to mute the unwanted notes.

Ready for another song? Let's try out the Everly Brothers' classic "Bye Bye Love" in the key of C. Besides pecking out the melody, we'll catch a few of the classic bass-string runs as well, which really help to goose the momentum when heading into the chorus.

BYE BYE LOVE

Words and Music by Felice Bryant and Boudleaux Bryant

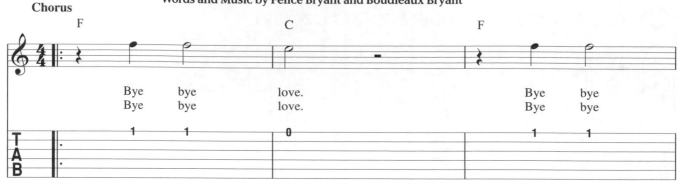

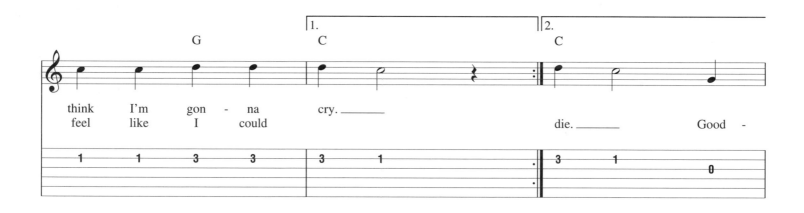

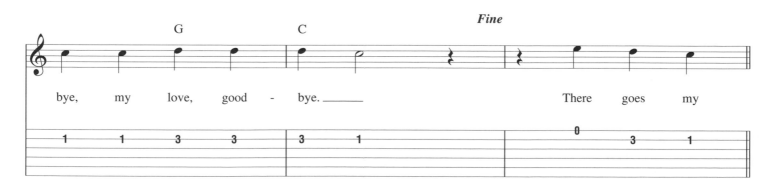

ba - by   with   some - one   new.

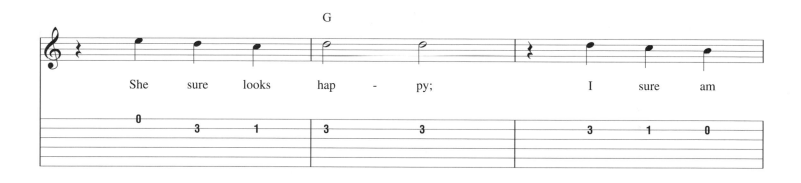

She   sure   looks   hap - py;   I   sure   am

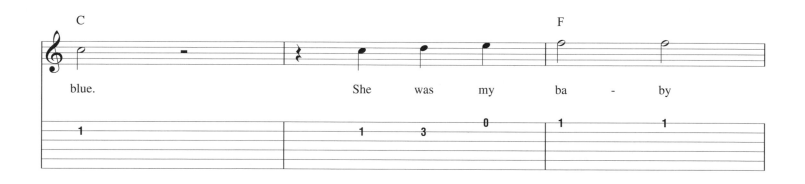

blue.   She   was   my   ba - by

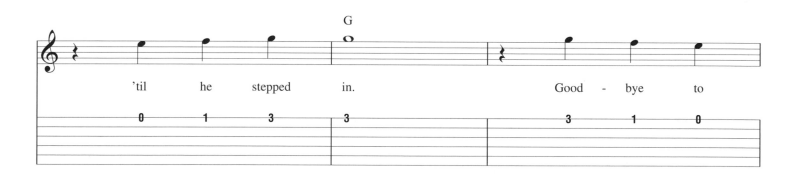

'til   he   stepped   in.   Good - bye   to

D.C. al Fine

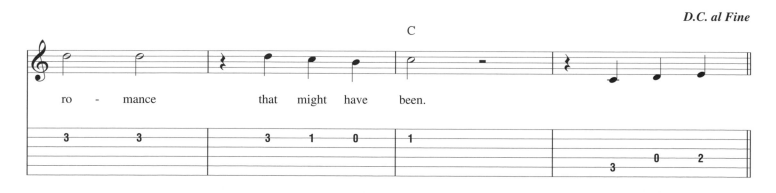

ro - mance   that   might   have   been.

CHAPTER 4: E Minor Pentatonic and C Major Scales   **49**

CHAPTER 5: 16TH NOTES

Strumming eighth notes can only take you so far on the guitar, so it's about time we tried our hand at some 16th notes. The good news is, although they may seem a little scary at first, the mechanics are no different than strumming eighth notes; it's just happening faster!

Let's start by analyzing a strum pattern containing quarter notes and eighth notes. Notice that downstrokes are used on the downbeats, and upstrokes are used on the upbeats. Therefore, your hand is continually moving down and up on every beat.

STRUMMING EIGHTH NOTES

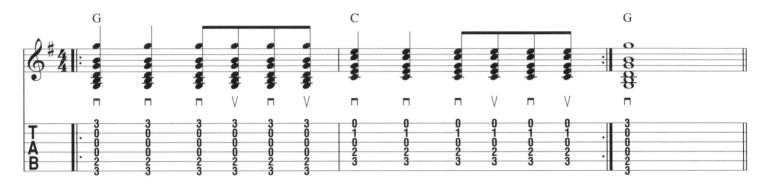

When strumming a 16th-note pattern though, we tend to move our picking hand down with every eighth note. The good news is that songs based on 16th notes tend to be slower in tempo than those based on eighth notes. So, even though the strumming mechanics are the same, it's not like taking the previous example and just playing it twice as fast. The number of strums per beat is increased, but the tempo usually decreases, so we get a break (usually).

Try this example now, paying attention to the strumming indicators. You're playing the same exact thing as the previous example, only a bit faster (not twice as fast, though, because the tempo has decreased). We count 16th notes as follows: 1-e-&-a, 2-e-&-a, etc.

STRUMMING 16TH NOTES

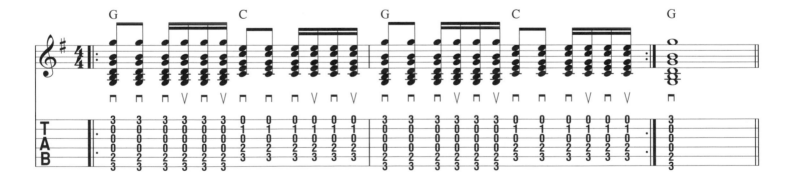

Why So Many Downstrokes?

When playing the previous example, you may have been tempted to use an upstroke for the second strum on each chord (beats 1.5 and 3.5). Though you could do this, I wouldn't recommend it, as it doesn't help you develop a good, consistent strumming feel. If you get in the habit of continuously moving your pick hand at the same speed (down on every beat for eighth-note-based songs and down on every eighth note for 16th note-based songs), you'll eventually be able to create all sorts of syncopated variations just by purposefully "missing" some strums and connecting with others.

Your pick hand is the timekeeper, so you want to try to get it on a certain "autopilot" with regard to down-and-upstrokes. You don't want to have to think about which direction to strum, because you'll eventually encounter all kinds of rhythms. If you develop the habit of pairing downstrokes with beats when strumming eighth notes and pairing downstrokes with eighth notes when strumming 16th notes, you'll never have to worry about strum direction again.

Let's take a look at a few examples that use some 16th notes in their strumming pattern. Be sure to follow the picking indicators!

ROOTS ROCK

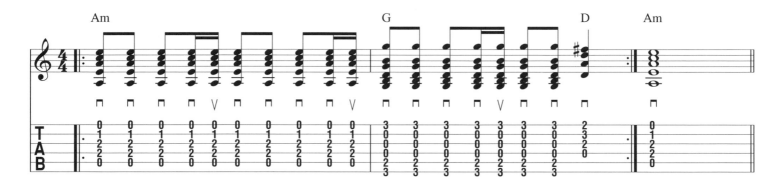

WIDE OPEN STRUMMING

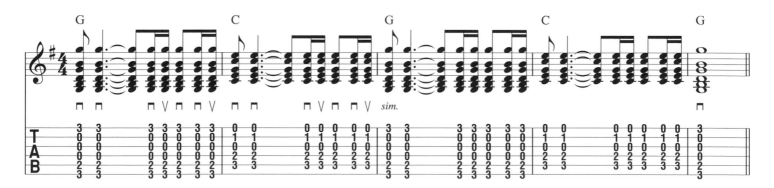

HURRY UP AND WAIT

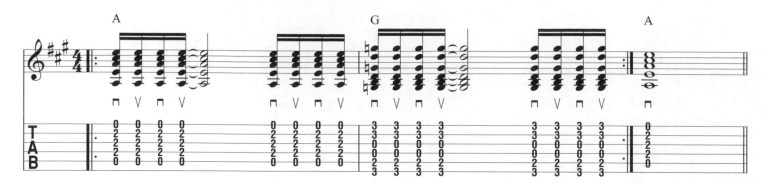

Remember the open-string cheat we talked about on page 33! You'll definitely need to make use of it during some of these 16th-note changes. You can especially hear it being used in the example above.

Now let's try out some 16th-note strumming on a few songs. The first one is Coldplay's "Yellow." We've transposed it to the key of G here and will be using four different chords: G, D, C, and Em.

YELLOW

Words and Music by Guy Berryman, Jon Buckland, Will Champion and Chris Martin

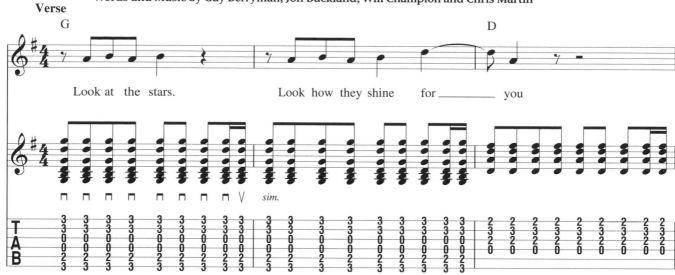

Look at the stars. Look how they shine for _____ you

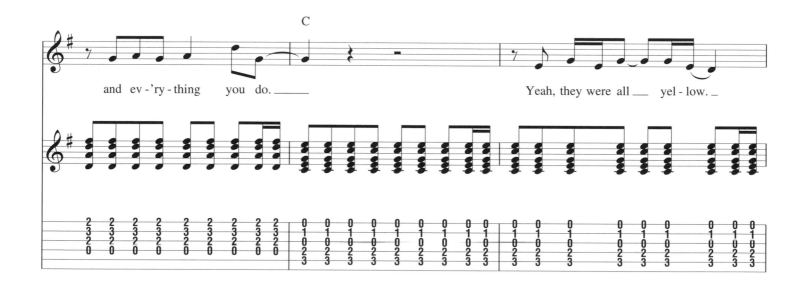

and ev-'ry-thing you do. _____ Yeah, they were all ___ yel-low. ___

I came a-long; I wrote a song for _____ you

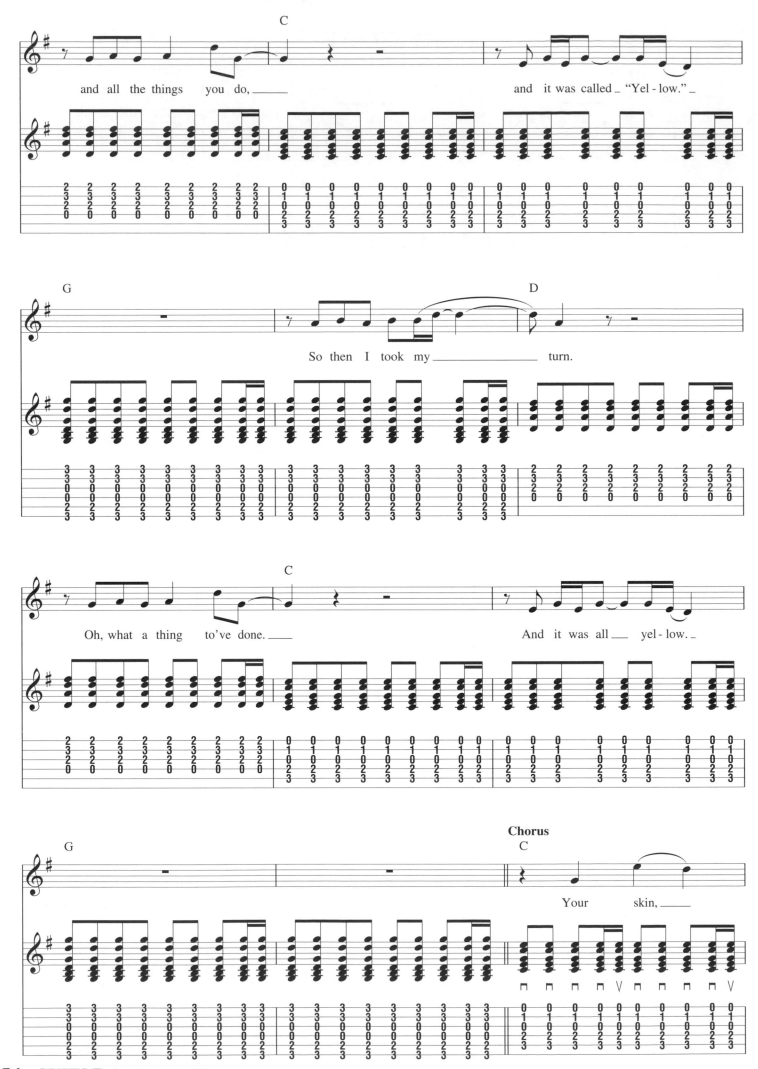

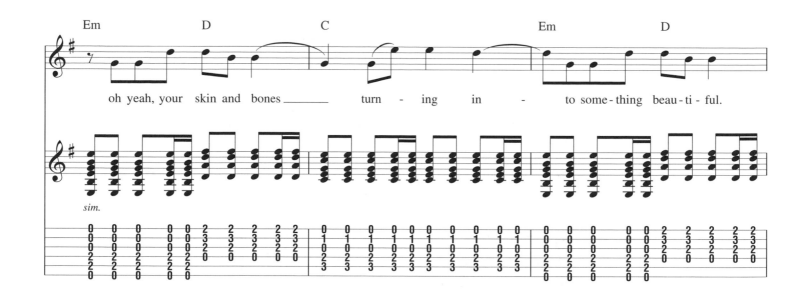

oh yeah, your skin and bones _____ turn - ing in - to some-thing beau-ti - ful.

D'you __ know, _____ you know I love you so? _____

You know I love you so. _____

And let's check out another tune while we're at it! Sublime's "What I Got" consists of mostly two chords, with another 16th-note-based groove. This one makes use of another new rhythm: the *dotted eighth note*. This is the same as an eighth note tied to a 16th note. Watch the picking indicators!

WHAT I GOT

Words and Music by Brad Nowell, Eric Wilson, Floyd Gaugh and Lindon Roberts

SCRATCH RHYTHM

Another technique that's often used on the uke—though often unconsciously—is referred to as *scratch rhythm* on the guitar. This describes the sound of muting all the strings with the fret hand and strumming them to produce a percussive, "clicking" sound. Simply lay your fret hand lightly across all the strings and strum them to hear the effect.

Try it out here, alternating a G chord with the muted strums. ("N.C." stands for "no chord.")

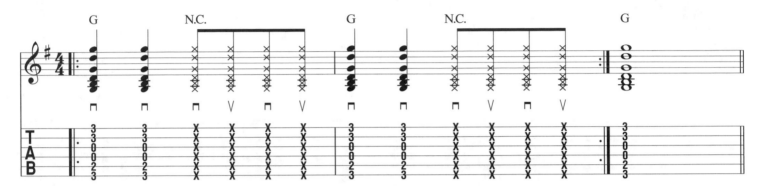

This is especially common with 16th-note strums. When you add a little syncopation, you can create a serious groove. Check it out in Bill Withers' "Use Me." The syncopated rhythm on the Em chords can be a little tricky at first, so take it slowly and listen to the audio until you get it down.

USE ME

Words and Music by Bill Withers

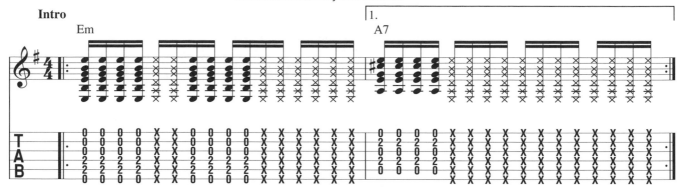

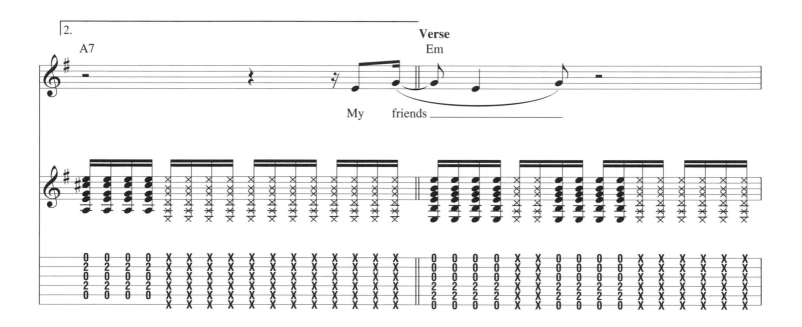

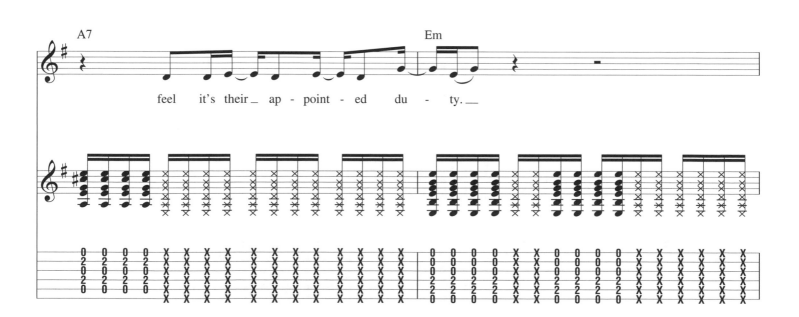

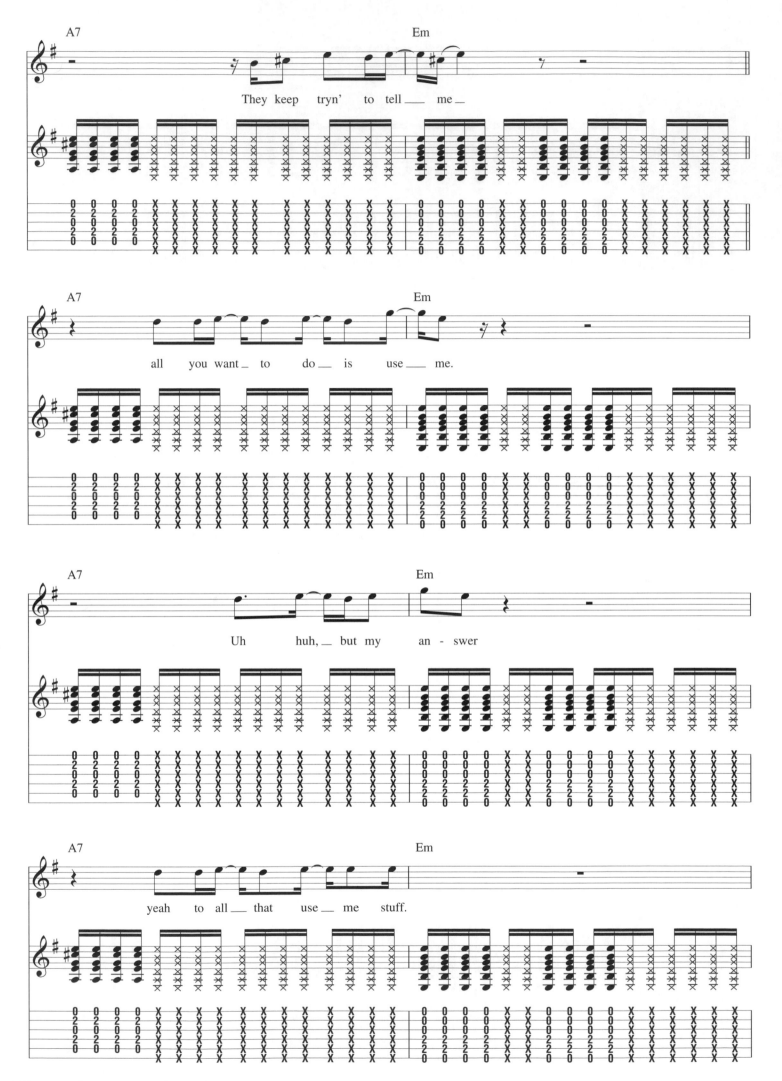

Chorus

I, ___ I, ___ I, ___ yes, uh, I _____ wan - na spread the news _ that if it feels _

___ this good _ get - tin' used, _ oh, ___ you just keep on us - ing me ___

un - til you use ___ me up. _____

CHAPTER 6: B7, E MAJOR, AND F♯ MINOR CHORDS

OK, let's add a few more chords. The first is B7.

B7

Like D7 and A7, B7 is a dominant chord. Place your second finger on fret 2, string 5, your first finger on fret 1, string 4, your third finger on fret 2, string 3, and your fourth finger on fret 2, string 1. Strum strings 5–1.

B7

2 1 3 4

You'll recognize this as the E7 chord shape on the uke:

E7

Let's check out B7 in this example. A few things to notice:

The second finger remains on the same string and fret in both the Em and B7 chords, so it's a great guide when changing between them.

The strum pattern uses a new syncopation. Follow the picking indicators. Keep your pick hand moving down on the beats and purposefully "miss" the strum (represented by the downstroke symbol in parentheses) on beat 3 to create the syncopation.

Em AND B7 WALK INTO A BAR LINE

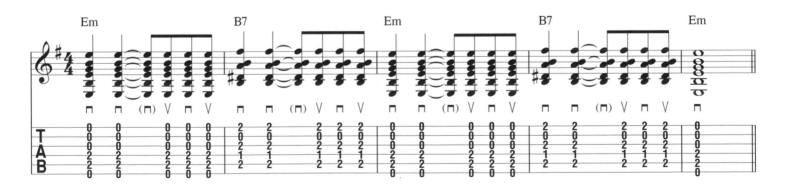

THE PERCUSSIVE PALM PLANT

Another technique that's used on guitar more often than realized is the *percussive palm plant*. It's not some rare form of vegetation from Hawaii; it's just a nice little technique to add a bit of rhythm to your chord playing. Here's how it works: Begin a downward strum motion as normal, but instead of strumming through the strings, forcefully plant your pick-hand palm on the strings to create a percussive "tick" sound.

Listen to the audio to hear what it sounds like:

You can place the percussive palm plant on beats 2 and 4 of an eighth-note strum pattern to simulate a snare drum. This is especially effective when you're playing by yourself. Your hand will still be moving down and up with each beat, but on beats 2 and 4, you'll plant your palm on the strings, making sure to land with the pick below the strings, and then continue with an upstroke.

ONE-MAN BAND

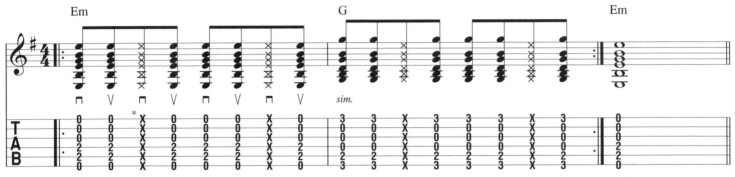

*Plant pick-hand palm on strings.

The percussive palm plant can also be used in 16th-note strum patterns. Remember that your pick hand is moving down every eighth note here.

ONE-MAN BAND: THE SEQUEL

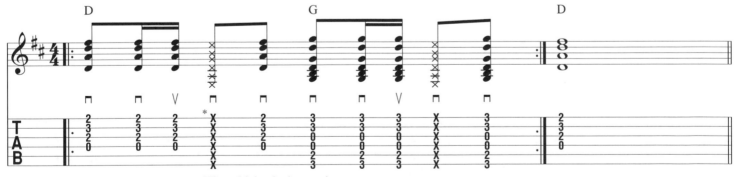

*Plant pick-hand palm on strings.

OK, now let's see how we can make use of this idea in a song. We've transposed Weezer's "Say It Ain't So" to the key of G (or E minor if you prefer), and we'll tackle it with Em, B7, C, and G chords. Instead of the palm plant appearing on beats 2 and 4, it's only appearing on beat 2 here. As this is a 16th-note-based strum pattern, remember that your pick hand should be moving down on every eighth note. In the chorus, be sure to mute those strings during the rests, as it adds to the musical drama!

SAY IT AIN'T SO

Words and Music by Rivers Cuomo

Intro

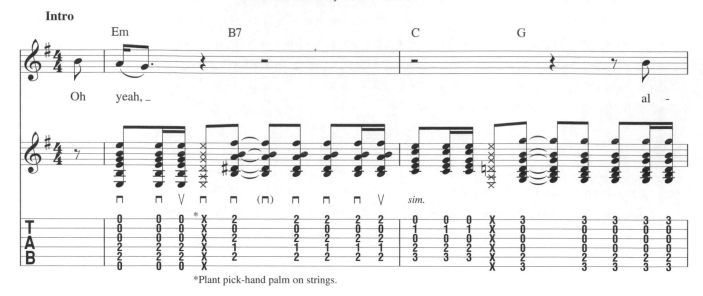

*Plant pick-hand palm on strings.

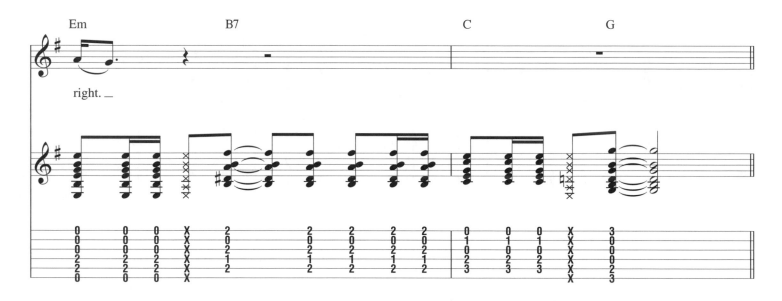

Verse

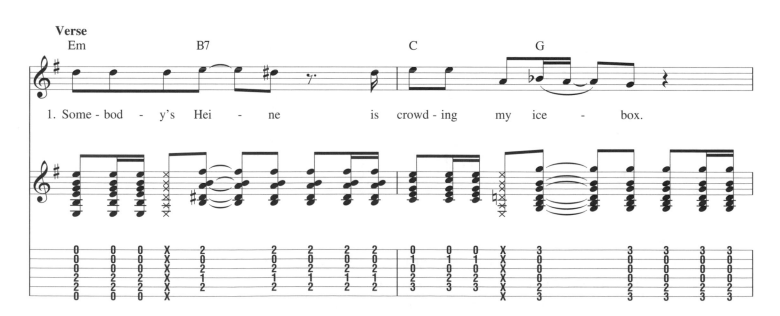

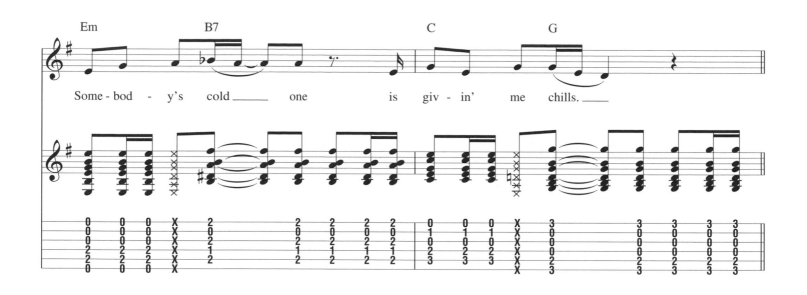

Some - bod - y's cold ___ one is giv - in' me chills. ___

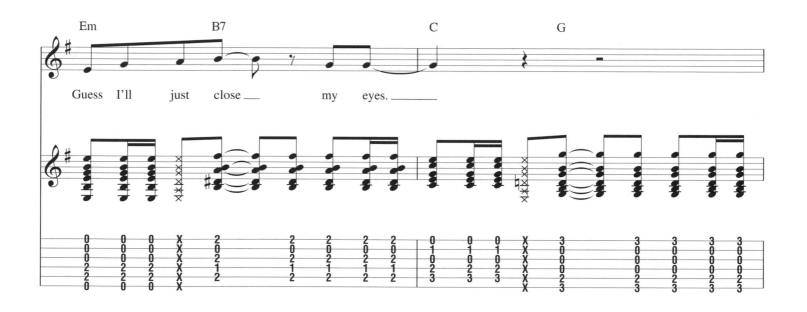

Guess I'll just close ___ my eyes. ___

Flip on the tel - ly, wres - tle with Jim - my.

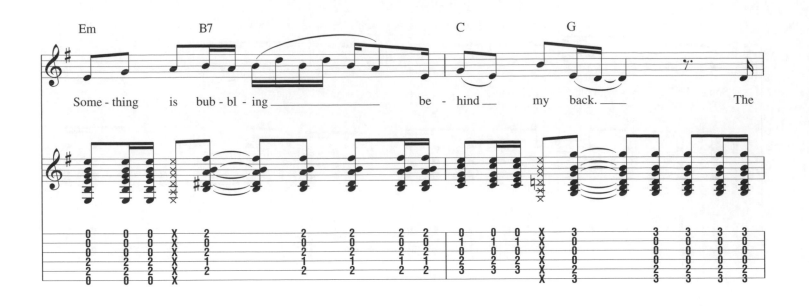

Some - thing is bub - bl - ing ____ be - hind ____ my back. ____ The

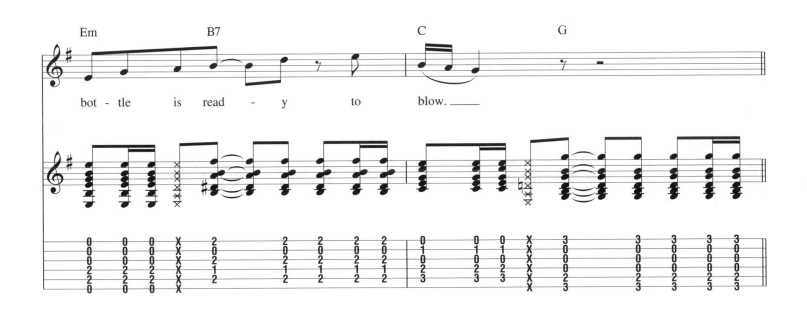

bot - tle is read - y to blow. ____

Chorus

Say it ain't so. ____

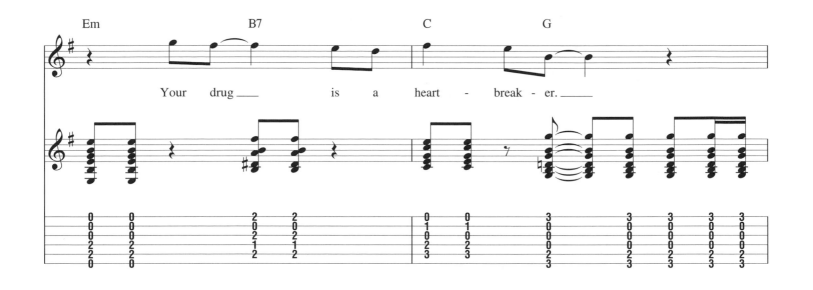

Your drug ____ is a heart - break - er. ____

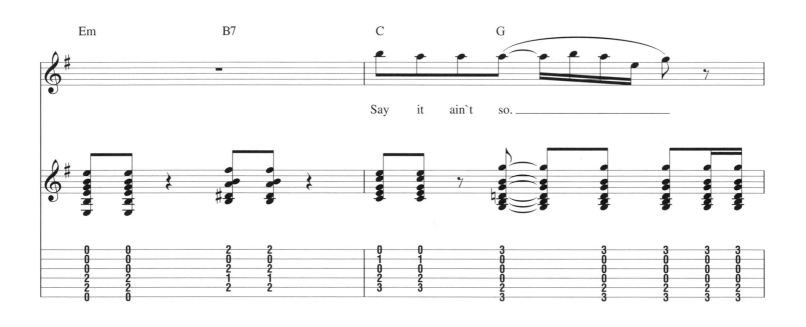

Say it ain`t so. _____

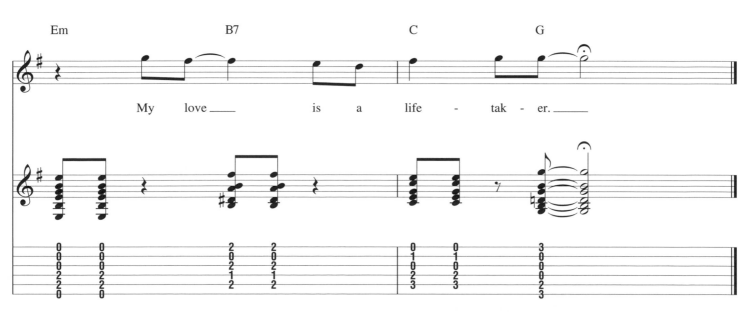

My love ____ is a life - tak - er. ____

Great! Let's check out some more chords now.

E MAJOR (E)

E major is a pretty easy chord. Place your second finger on fret 2, string 5, your third finger on fret 2, string 4, and your first finger on fret 1, string 3. Strum all six strings.

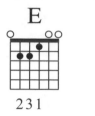

2 3 1

You'll recognize this one as the A major chord shape on the uke:

Let's try out the E chord in another strumming example. This one continues expanding on our syncopated strum patterns. Again, keep that pick hand moving down on every beat in this eighth-note-based pattern.

EDA A. STRUMMER

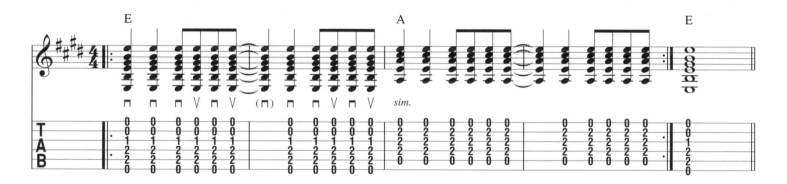

Let's try another variation. One common guitar strumming technique, especially in more jangly, country-inspired styles, involves playing the lowest note of the chord on beat 1 and then strumming the chord on beats 2 and 4. You should use all downstrokes here.

JANGLY BRITISH ROCK

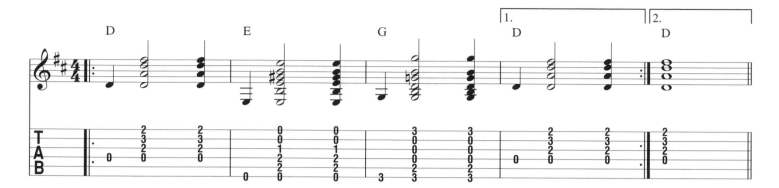

And here's another new chord!

F♯ MINOR (F♯m)

This one is a bit more difficult because you're required to hold down several strings with one finger. Technically, this makes it a "barre chord," but it's not what most people mean when they talk about barre chords on the guitar. They normally involve five or all six strings. Place your third finger on fret 4, string 4 and use your first finger to hold down strings 3, 2, and 1 at fret 2. Strum strings 4 thru 1.

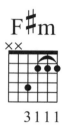

You'll recognize this shape as Bm on the uke:

Let's try out F♯m here. Be sure to notice that your third finger can act as a guide when moving from E back to F♯m as it remains on string 4.

SAD STRUMMER

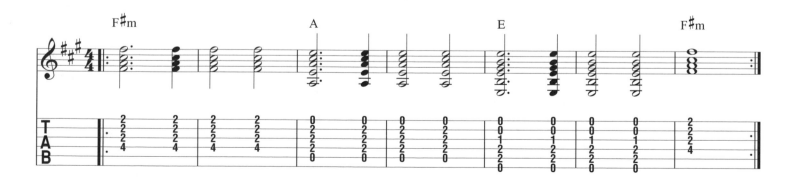

Let's try out a few of these new chords in another song. The Jason Mraz hit "I'm Yours" features a strong upbeat feel, which gives it a slight island or reggae sound. We'll emulate that with our strum pattern. In the chorus, we're applying a *palm mute* ("P.M.") to get a muted sound. Lay your palm on the strings, just in front of bridge as you strum the strings. The farther in from the bridge, you move, the more muted the sound becomes. We're after a moderate mute here.

I'M YOURS

Words and Music by Jason Mraz

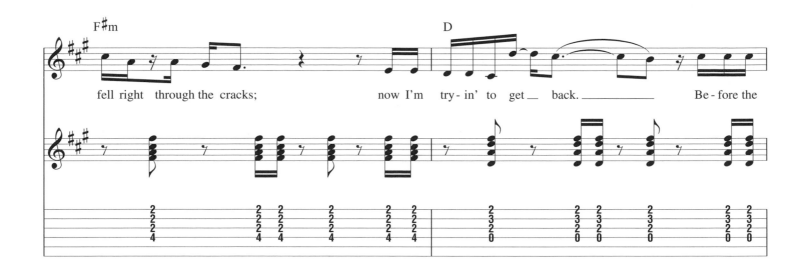

fell right through the cracks;   now I'm try-in' to get __ back. _____ Be - fore the

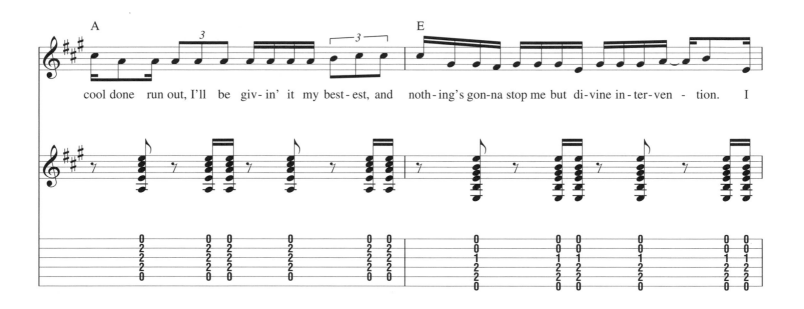

cool done run out, I'll be giv-in' it my best-est, and noth-ing's gon-na stop me but di-vine in-ter-ven - tion.   I

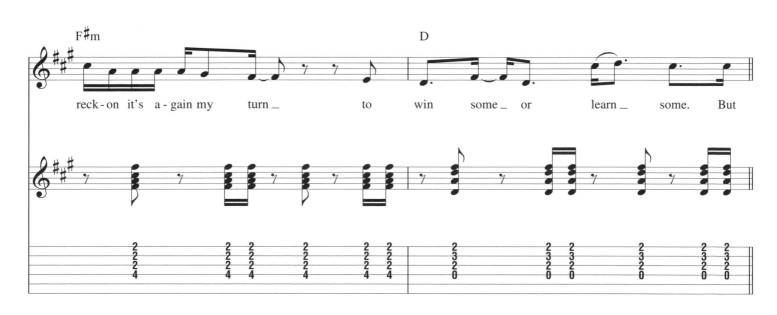

reck-on it's a-gain my turn __ to win some __ or learn __ some. But

I ___ won't hes - i - tate no more, ___ no

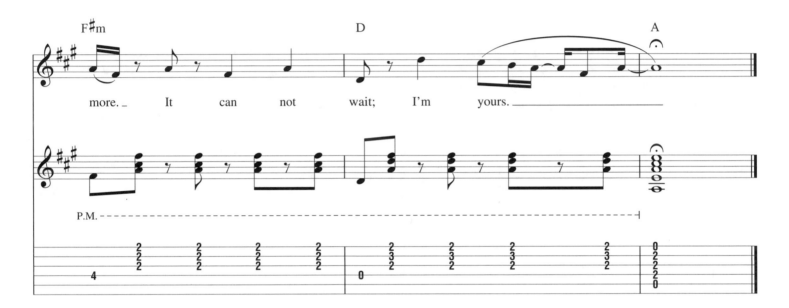

more. ___ It can not wait; I'm yours. ___

Alright, let's switch gears and get back to playing some melodies. We're going to play the Beatles' classic "Get Back" in the key of C. Before we do, though, we need to look at two notes that aren't in the C major scale; these are sometimes referred to as "blue notes."

The note B♭ appears on fret 3, string 3. Use your third finger for this note.

B♭ note

And E♭ appears on fret 1, string 4. Use your first finger for this note.

E♭ note

GET BACK

Words and Music by John Lennon and Paul McCartney

Verse

1. Jo - jo was a man who thought __ he was a lon - er but ____ he knew it could - n't last. __

__ Jo - jo left his home in Tus - son, Ar - i - zon - a for __

__ some Cal - i - for - nia grass. __ Get back, __ get back, __ get back __

Chorus

__ to where you once be - longed. __ Get back, __ get back, __ get back

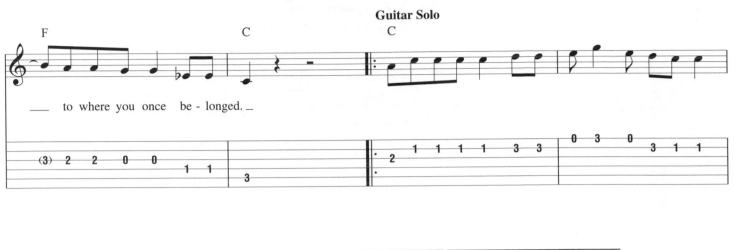

to where you once be - longed. _

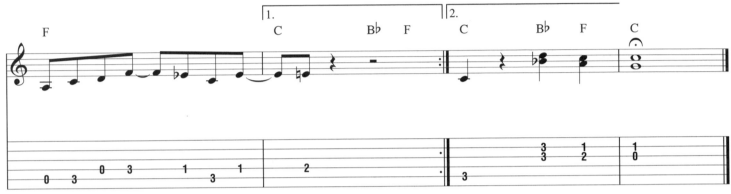

Chapter 7: B Minor and F Major Chords and Arpeggios

Let's add two more chords for good measure before we wrap things up.

B MINOR (Bm)

For Bm, place your third finger on fret 4, string 4, your fourth finger on fret 4, string 3, your second finger on fret 3, string 2, and your first finger on fret 2, string 1. Strum strings 4 thru 1. With a little practice, you can use the tip of your third finger to keep string 5 quiet and bring your thumb over the top to mute string 6 if necessary.

Bm

3 4 2 1

This chord should remind you of an Em chord shape on the uke:

Em

Let's hear how the Bm chord sounds in "Iris" by the Goo Goo Dolls. This song is another one in 12/8 meter (see page 29), but this time we're adding a few 16th notes to the strums. Your pick hand should be moving down on every eighth note. Watch the strum indicators at first to get the feel.

IRIS

From the Motion Picture CITY OF ANGELS
Words and Music by John Rzeznik

Chorus

And I don't want the world to see me 'cause I

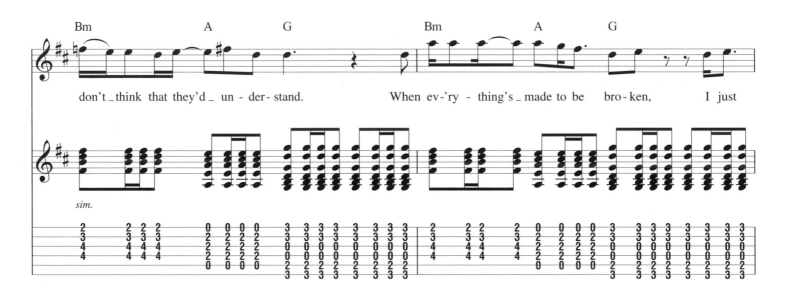

don't think that they'd under-stand. When ev'ry-thing's made to be bro-ken, I just

want you to know who I am.

F MAJOR (F)

For the F chord, place your third finger on fret 3, string 4, your second finger on fret 2, string 3, and use your first finger to play strings 2 and 1 at fret 1. Strum strings 4 thru 1. Just like the F#m chord, you can use the tip of your third finger to mute string 5 and the thumb to mute string 6 if necessary.

You know this shape as B♭ on the uke:

Let's check out the F chord in Traffic's "Feelin' Alright." The strum pattern here is the trickiest yet, so look at it very closely. It includes a syncopated 16th note, so you'll need to follow the picking indicators very closely and listen to the audio to make sure you've got a feel for it. Since it's a 16th-note pattern, your pick hand should be moving down on every eighth note.

FEELIN' ALRIGHT

Words and Music by Dave Mason

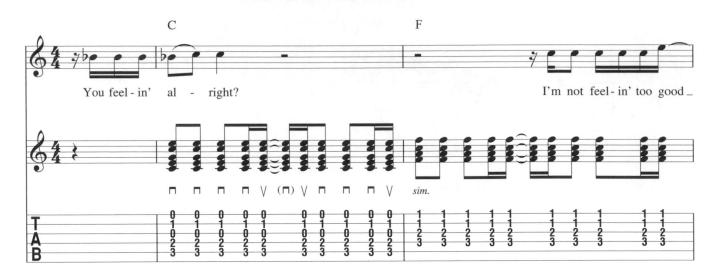

You feel-in' al - right? I'm not feel-in' too good _

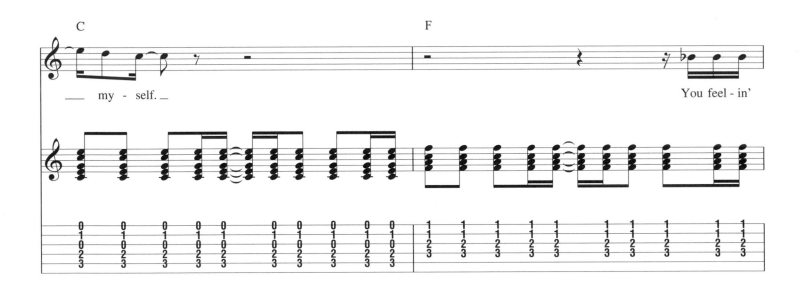

_ my - self. _ You feel - in'

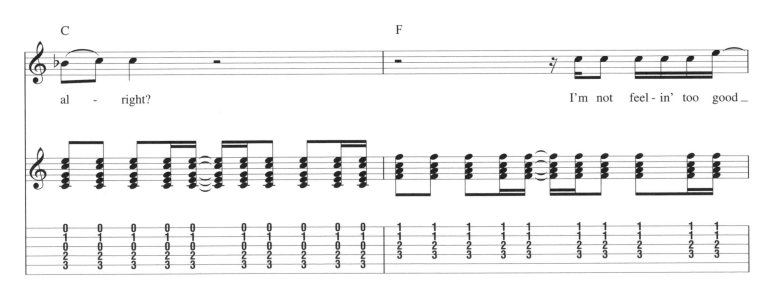

al - right? I'm not feel-in' too good _

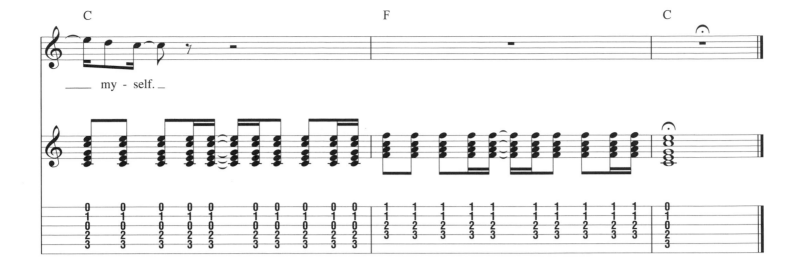

ARPEGGIOS

We'll close out with another great guitar technique, called arpeggios. An *arpeggio* is simply a chord played as individual notes, one after the other. However, unlike strumming, the direction of your pick strokes is not standardized with arpeggios; it's usually dictated more by whatever is easiest and/or what feels most natural to you, depending on the tempo and the busyness of the part, among other things.

Check out the basic idea here in the key of C:

PICKIN' AND GRINNIN'

Notice, on the G chord, we skipped the fifth string. This type of thing happens often in arpeggio pattern so you have to be on the lookout. Let's hear how it sounds when applied to a real song. The Bruno Mars song "Moonshine" sounds great with arpeggios. Although this is recorded with an electric guitar, it'll sound nice with an acoustic guitar, as well.

MOONSHINE

Words and Music by Bruno Mars, Ari Levine, Philip Lawrence, Jeff Bhasker, Andrew Wyatt and Mark Ronson

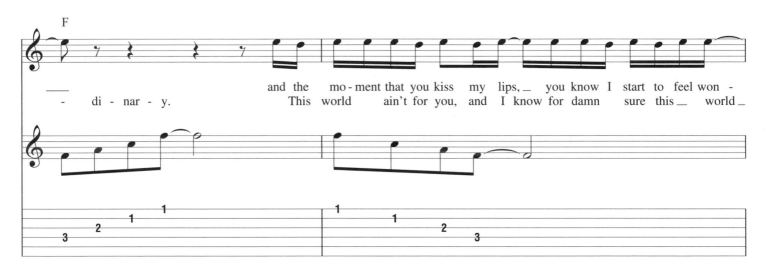

1.

Am   G

sex   in   your   chem - i - cals,   oh. _____   Let's go____

2.

Am   G

Just   let   your   fire   set   me   free. ____   Oh, _____

Chorus

Am

moon -   shine,   take   us   to   the

stars to - night. _____ Take us to that

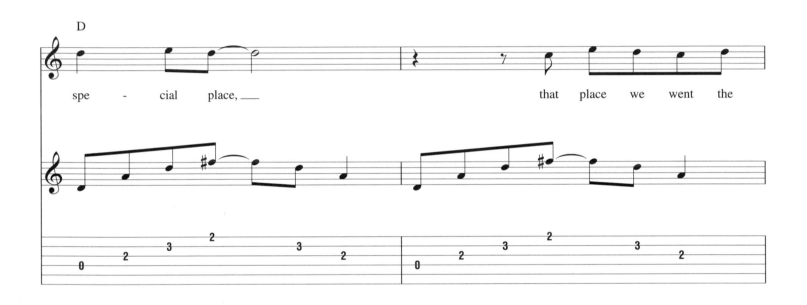

spe - cial place, _____ that place we went the

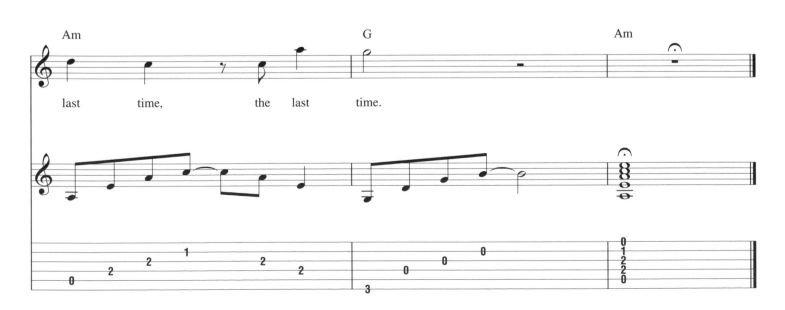

last time, the last time.

APPENDIX

Hello there! Thanks for stopping by the Appendix. That's mighty thorough of you.

GUITAR/UKULELE CHORD CONVERSION CHART

As I mentioned in the book, all the chord shapes on the uke are transferable to the guitar's top four strings; they just have different names. The following chart illustrates that connection with some of the most common chords. We learned most of these in the book, but not all of them. So it's a good thing you came here!

Guitar	Ukulele		Guitar	Ukulele		Guitar	Ukulele
C	F	=	Am	Dm	=	B7	E7
A	D	=	F#m	Bm	=	A7	D7
G	C	=	Em	Am	=	E7	A7
E	A	=	Dm	Gm	=	D7	G7
D	G	=	Bm	Em	=	F#7	B7
F	B♭	=					

NOTES ON THE GUITAR FRETBOARD

This diagram shows you the names of all the notes on the guitar fretboard. After fret 12, they start all over again an octave higher. For instance, fret 13 on string 6 is F, fret 14 is F♯/G♭, etc.

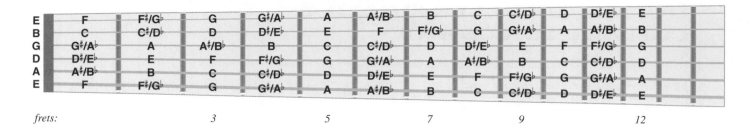

frets: 3   5   7   9   12

COMMON SCALE FINGERINGS

We learned a few scales in the book, but there are many more, as you may know from your uke studies. Here's a selection of some of the most commonly used scales on the guitar. These shapes are moveable to any key.

Major (Ionian)

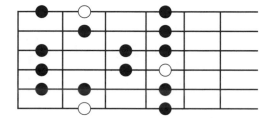

Minor (Aeolian)

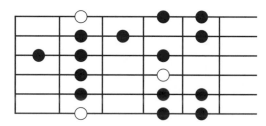

Major (Pentatonic)

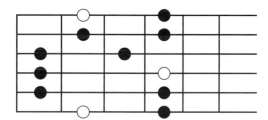

Minor (Pentatonic)

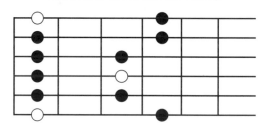

Mixolydian

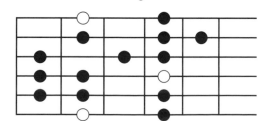

Dorian

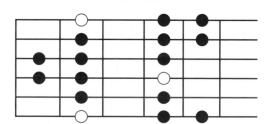

Harmonic Minor

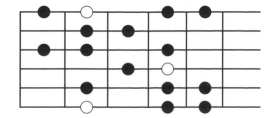

Melodic Minor

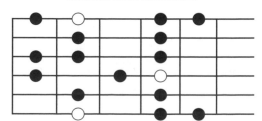

BLANK CHORD GRIDS AND TAB PAPER

Make copies of these pages so when you learn any cool new chords, scales, licks, or riffs, you'll have somewhere to write them!

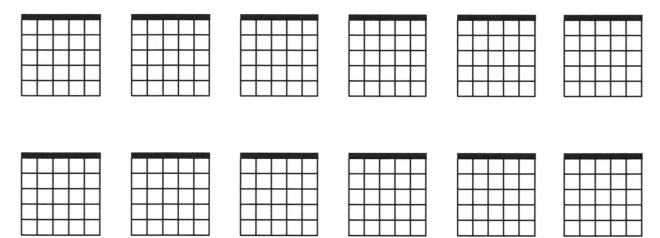

TAB

T
A
B